Unterrichtsmodell

Series Editor: Hans Kröger

Tennessee Williams

A Streetcar Named Desire

by Michael Groschwald

EinFach Englisch

Schöningh

Vorwort

Einzelarbeit

Partnerarbeit

Gruppen-
arbeit

Unterrichts-
gespräch

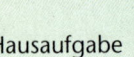

Schreib-
auftrag

Hausaufgabe

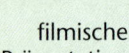

filmische
Präsentation

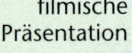

Projekt, offene
Aufgabe

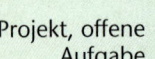

kreative
Aufgabe

szenisches
Spiel,
Rollenspiel

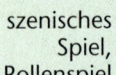

Der Titel der Reihe **EinFach Englisch** verdeutlicht Zielsetzung und Programm zugleich. Einerseits soll Schülerinnen und Schülern auf einfache Art und Weise der Zugang zu klassischen, aber auch neuen literarischen Werken und Filmen ermöglicht werden, andererseits sollen Lehrerinnen und Lehrern in der Praxis erprobte Unterrichtsmodelle angeboten werden, die die wichtigsten methodisch-didaktischen Ansätze ihres Faches Englisch abdecken. Dabei sind die Modelle direkt, ohne langes Einlesen einsetzbar und stellen Unterrichtsarbeit konkret vor. Als besonders hilfreich für die Praxis haben sich dabei folgende Aspekte erwiesen, die für die Gestaltung der Reihe wesentlich sind:

- Überblick über **Figurenkonstellation**, ggf. **Filmszenen** und **Inhalt**
- **Klausuren** mit **Erwartungshorizont**
- **Arbeitsblätter**, **Tafelbilder** und **Leitfragen** für den Unterricht
- **Piktogramme** als Hinweise auf **Unterrichts-** und **Arbeitsformen**

Das Prinzip der „**Components**" ermöglicht darüber hinaus den variablen Einsatz der Modelle in unterschiedlich konzipierten Unterrichtsreihen. Dabei stehen Machbarkeit und Praxisnähe stets im Vordergrund.

Das vorliegende Modell bezieht sich auf folgende Textausgabe:
Tennessee Williams, *A Streetcar Named Desire*, hrsg. v. Herbert Geisen, Reclam, Stuttgart 2003, ISBN 978-3-15-009240-8

Sprachliche Betreuung: Simone Duxbury-Ziemer

Bildnachweis: S. 3: © defd; S. 9: © ullstein bild – Lebrecht Music & Arts Photo Library

© 2008 Bildungshaus Schulbuchverlage
Westermann Schroedel Diesterweg Schöningh Winklers GmbH
Braunschweig, Paderborn, Darmstadt

www.schoeningh-schulbuch.de
Schöningh Verlag, Jühenplatz 1 – 3, 33098 Paderborn

Druck 5 4 3 2 1 / Jahr 2012 11 10 09 08
Die letzte Zahl bezeichnet das Jahr dieses Druckes.

Umschlaggestaltung: Peter und Veronika Wypior
Umschlagabbildung: © defd
Druck und Bindung: westermann druck GmbH, Braunschweig

ISBN 978-3-14-041238-4

Getting started

1. Describe the two people in the photo.

2. What do their postures reveal about their state of mind and the situation they are in?

3. In what way might the two persons be related to each other?

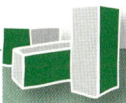

Die Personen

Blanche DuBois

Das Leben der einer ebenso kultivierten wie dekadenten Südstaatenfamilie entstammenden Englischlehrerin Blanche DuBois ist in eine schier unentrinnbare Sackgasse eingemündet. Auf der Flucht vor einer Vergangenheit, die von der Mitschuld am Tod ihres homosexuellen Mannes, der Verführung eines minderjährigen Schülers sowie zügelloser Promiskuität überschattet ist, sieht sich die sensible, verletzliche und flatterhafte Blanche im Haus ihrer Schwester Stella mit der Kulturlosigkeit, Rohheit und Kompromisslosigkeit von deren Ehemann Stanley konfrontiert. Obschon sie Stanleys dominantes Gebaren mit einer Mischung aus Koketterie, Ironie und Überheblichkeit zu karikieren bzw. diskreditieren sucht, wird schon in der ersten Szene des Dramas offensichtlich, dass Blanche zu viele Angriffsflächen bietet, um sich auf Dauer gegen Stanleys Brutalität und Verschlagenheit behaupten zu können. Ihre unangemessen glamouröse Kleidung, ihre nervöse Überspanntheit, ihre ungeschickten Versuche, ihre Trunksucht und ihr Alter zu kaschieren sowie ihre vermeintliche Mitschuld am Verlust des Familienanwesens Belle Reve stempeln sie in einer durch rationale Ordnungsprinzipien und archaische Lebensmuster geprägten Welt zu einer mit Argwohn beäugten Außenseiterin. Blanches akademischer bzw. aristokratischer Dünkel und die hiermit einhergehende Unfähigkeit zu erkennen, dass weder ihre mit Überheblichkeit zur Schau gestellte Bildung noch ihr exaltierter Ästhetizismus dazu angetan sind, Einfluss auf das kleinbürgerliche und kulturlose Leben Stellas und Stanleys zu nehmen, führt schließlich zur Katastrophe. In Verkennung des unbedingten und radikalen Machtanspruchs, welchen Stanley über seine proletarische Welt erhebt, wird Blanche zur Verliererin bzw. zum Opfer eines von ihr fahrlässig entfachten Klassenkampfes. Blanches Vergewaltigung durch Stanley, welche schließlich auf Betreiben Stellas zu ihrer Einlieferung in eine Nervenheilanstalt führt, ist somit nicht nur als persönliche Tragödie zu verstehen, sondern darüber hinaus auch als eine Metapher für den Niedergang einer anachronistischen Idealen nachhängenden Südstaatenaristokratie, die sich in einem auf Pragmatismus und Rationalismus ausgerichteten Amerika nicht mehr zu behaupten vermag.

Stanley Kowalski

Stanley Kowalski, ein ca. 30-jähriger amerikanischer Fabrikarbeiter mit polnischen Wurzeln, ist die Inkarnation verwegener Virilität und rauer Manneskraft. Pfauengleich und voller Selbstzufriedenheit bewegt sich Stanley in einem Milieu, in dem Kraftmeierei und Machismo mit Akzeptanz und Anerkennung quittiert werden. In der Gewissheit, dass sowohl seine Frau Stella als auch seine Freunde ihm mit unerschütterlicher Loyalität und Ehrerbietung begegnen, schwingt sich Stanley zum uneingeschränkten Herrscher seines kleinbürgerlichen bzw. proletarischen Mikrokosmos auf. Folglich gerät seine dominante Position auch nicht in Gefahr, als Stellas Schwester Blanche versucht, ihn zu diskreditieren bzw. als Affen und Steinzeitmenschen zu diffamieren. In seiner Eitelkeit verletzt, und getrieben von einem nagenden Misstrauen gegenüber dem von Blanche verkörperten Bildungsbürgertum, geht Stanley mit aller ihm zur Verfügung stehenden Brutalität und Verschlagenheit gegen die fragile und flatterhafte Englischlehrerin vor. Die in einer Vergewaltigung mündende Unterjochung und seelische Zerstörung Blanches entspringt jedoch nicht nur leidenschaftlichen Rachegelüsten Stanleys, sondern ist in erster Linie Ausdruck seiner tief empfundener Respektlosigkeit bzw. Verachtung gegenüber Frauen. Unter diesem Blickwinkel müssen auch die leidenschaftlichen bzw. hysterischen Beteuerungen betrachtet werden, mittels derer es Stanley gelingt, die sich mehrmals von ihm abwendende Stella zurückzugewinnen. Stanleys emotionale Ausbrüche sind weder Ausdruck selbstloser Liebe noch Zeichen tiefer Zärtlichkeit, sondern sie sind vielmehr Mechanismen, die dazu dienen sich (s)eine Frau gefügig zu machen.

Mitch

Der scheue und introvertierte Junggeselle Mitch ist ein Arbeitskollege Stanley Kowalskis und regelmäßiger Teilnehmer an den in Stanleys Wohnung stattfindenden Pokerrunden. Als Mitch in rührend unbeholfener Weise beginnt, Stanleys Schwägerin Blanche zu hofieren, verkörpert er zunächst den lang ersehnten Rettungsanker für Blanches aus dem Ruder gelaufene Existenz, wird jedoch schließlich unbewusst und ungewollt zum Auslöser für deren Persönlichkeitszerstörung. Gefangen im starren Korsett kleinbürgerlicher Moralvorstellungen und somit unfähig die tieferen Beweggründe für Blanches innere Zerrissenheit und Frivolität zu erkennen, wendet er sich voller Ekel und Verachtung von dieser ab, als Stanley – getrieben durch Eifersucht und Missgunst – pikante Details aus deren Vergangenheit offenbart. Sowohl Mitchs fehlschlagender Versuch, Blanche als Zeichen seiner Verachtung zu vergewaltigen, als auch seine Unfähigkeit, zu erkennen, dass er Stanley, welcher Blanche schließlich „erfolgreich" zum Beischlaf zwingt, nur als Claqueur und Bewunderer dient, machen ihn zum passiven und willfährigen Werkzeug in den Händen des Protagonisten Stanley und stempeln ihn gleichsam zu dessen bloßem Gegenentwurf.

Stella

Stella, die wie ihre Schwester Blanche einer vornehmen und traditionsreichen Südstaatenfamilie entstammt, teilt weder den Standesdünkel noch die Exaltiertheit ihrer Schwester. Anstatt dessen assimiliert sie sich den Gepflogenheiten der kleinbürgerlichen Welt ihres Mannes Stanley und begegnet darüber hinaus dessen Impulsivität und Aggressivität mit einem auffallend hohen Maß an Toleranz. Obschon sie aus Empörung und Wut über Stanleys körperliche Übergriffe gelegentlich Zuflucht bei ihrer Nachbarin Eunice sucht, ist sie ihrem Mann mit leidenschaftlicher Liebe zugetan. Dies wird besonders deutlich, als Blanche – welcher Stella mit einer Mischung aus respektvoller Rücksichtnahme und ironischer Distanz begegnet – versucht, Stanley aufgrund seiner Gewalttätigkeit und Brutalität zu diffamieren. Anstatt auf Anraten ihrer Schwester dem proletarischen und kulturlosen Milieu ihres Mannes zu entfliehen, rechtfertigt Stella Stanleys rüdes Verhalten unter anderem mit dem Verweis auf die sexuelle Anziehungskraft, welche seine Aggressivität auf sie ausübt. Ob es schließlich sexuelle Hörigkeit ist oder eine bedingungslose Solidarisierung mit Stanley und dessen Umfeld, welche Stella dazu bewegen, einem Mann die Treue zu halten, der ihre Schwester vergewaltigt hat und somit verantwortlich ist für deren Einlieferung in eine Nervenheilanstalt, bleibt eine der zentralen und offenen Fragen, welche Williams Drama aufwirft.

Der Inhalt

Als Blanche DuBois, eine aus einer vornehmen und traditionsreichen Südstaatenfamilie stammende Englischlehrerin, auf der Flucht vor einer durch fragwürdige Machenschaften und Ereignisse geprägten Vergangenheit Unterschlupf im Haus ihrer Schwester Stella Kowalski findet, geben ihre nervöse Überspanntheit und ihre offensichtliche Alkoholabhängigkeit klare Hinweise darauf, dass ihr Leben aus den Fugen geraten ist. Ihre permanenten Versuche, ihr neues kleinbürgerlich bzw. proletarisch geprägtes Umfeld durch Bildung, Vornehmheit und Glamour zu beeindrucken, erweisen sich in der Folge als äußerst kontraproduktiv. Durch übertriebene Exaltiertheit und Koketterie das Misstrauen des gewalttätigen, seine Ehefrau Stella schlagenden Stanley Kowalski weckend, gerät Blanche auf dessen Druck in immer größere Konfusion und Erklärungsnot. So zwingt Stanley sie nicht nur dazu, den Verlust des Familienanwesens Belle Reve zu erklären bzw. zu dokumentieren, sondern enthüllt darüber hinaus auch dunkle Seiten ihrer Vergangenheit wie beispielsweise die Verführung eines minderjährigen Schülers und dem hiermit einhergehenden Verlust ihrer Stellung als Englischlehrerin.

Stanleys gnadenloses und unerbittliches Aufdecken von Blanches Fehltritten ist nicht nur durch das provokante sowie frivole Gebaren seiner Schwägerin motiviert, sondern gründet sich im Wesentlichen auf zwei entscheidenden Ereignissen bzw. Entwicklungen: Zum einen belauscht er Blanche bei dem Versuch, ihre Schwester Stella dazu zu bewegen, ihrem proletarischen Milieu zu entfliehen indem sie ihn (Stanley) als Untermenschen und Proleten diffamiert und zum anderen missbilligt er die sich anbahnende Beziehung zwischen Blanche und seinem Kollegen und alten Weggefährten Mitch. Indem Stanley seinem Freund, der sich ernsthaft mit dem Gedanken trägt, Blanche zu ehelichen, pikante Details aus deren Vergangenheit offenbart, zerstört er nicht nur dessen Hoffnung, nun endlich die Frau seines Lebens gefunden zu haben, sondern beginnt gleichzeitig damit, Blanche einer Reihe von Demütigungen auszusetzen, die schließlich in deren Vergewaltigung kulminieren.

Stella, die sich während der Vergewaltigung ihrer Schwester durch Stanley zur Entbindung von ihrem ersten Kind im Krankenhaus befindet, missbilligt zwar die gnadenlose Brutalität, mit welcher ihr Ehemann gegen Blanche vorgeht, vermag es jedoch nicht, diesem den Rücken zu kehren. Ihre Trauer, Empörung und Gewissenskonflikte angesichts der durch sie selbst veranlassten Einlieferung ihrer Schwester in eine Nervenheilanstalt schwinden förmlich dahin, als Stanley beginnt, sie mit Koseworten und Liebkosungen zu umgarnen.

The author

Thomas Lanier Williams was born on 26 March, 1911 in Columbus, Mississippi (the nickname *Tennessee* was given to him later at college by a fellow student who confused Tennessee with Mississippi). He was the eldest of the three children that resulted from the marriage between Cornelius Coffin Williams, an employee of a telephone company and Edwina Dakin, a spoilt, impractical Southern Belle. Since his parents had a rather bad marriage, Williams' childhood was overshadowed by feelings of insecurity and fear. His mother's propensity for turning her back on her husband and taking refuge in her parents' rectory as well as his father's fixation with his career, which finally enabled him to take up a managerial post in a shoe company in St. Louis, had a disastrous effect on Williams and his two younger siblings

Rose and Dakin. Being accustomed to the amenities of their grandparents' house and the simple pleasures of country life, the family's move to St. Louis not only exposed the children to the anonymity and complexity of urban life, but also forced them to cope with their mother's disappointment at being a non-entity in a large city.

While Williams found temporary solace in a trip to Europe that he embarked on with his grandfather, the Rev. Dakin, in 1928, his father's drinking bouts and the deteriorating condition of his feeble and ailing sister Rose started becoming a heavy burden on the family. During Williams' studies at the State University of Iowa, which he was able to take up in 1937 after having been forced by the Great Depression to temporarily put his academic career on hold and work in a shoe firm instead, things at home came to a head. Claiming that she had been sexually harassed by her father, his mentally-unstable sister Rose was made to undergo an operation called lobotomy, in the process of which parts of the brain are removed in order to treat mental problems. This particular incident and his inability to forgive his mother for her part in the whole affair affected Williams' personality and his work to a considerable degree. Accordingly, two of Williams' most renowned heroines (Blanche in *A Streetcar Named Desire* and Laura in *The Glass Menagerie*) bear striking resemblances to his sister Rose.

Although Williams' works contain a great number of themes (fate, desire, illness, the decadence and decay of the South, etc.) that are inextricably linked with his personal experiences, his plays never dealt explicitly with his homosexuality. Instead of taking up the cause of homosexuality like many other writers (e.g. Christopher Isherwood), Williams followed his own rules and turned out to be one of the most prolific and successful playwrights of his time. Nevertheless, although a considerable number of his plays were made into movies and thus guaranteed him wealth as well as independence, his success did not turn him into a happy man. On account of his drug addiction, alcoholism as well as a frenetic search for sexual encounters, he finally had to undergo psychotherapy for depression. Having started to write plays that were neither popular with theatre producers nor with the public and being weakened by his excessive lifestyle, the last twenty years of Williams' life were marked by dwindling success and several sojourns in mental hospitals. Having choked to death on one of his barbiturates, Williams died in New York on 24 February, 1983 in a hotel called the Elysée (a name ironically evocative of the *Elysian Fields* in *A Streetcar Named Desire*). Williams' literary achievements gained him a considerable number of prizes and awards, among them the Pulitzer Prize for *A Streetcar Named Desire* (1948) and *Cat on a Hot Tin Roof (1955).*

The dramas *The Glass Menagerie* (1945) and *The Night of the Iguana* (1961) gained him the New York Drama Critics' Circle Award.

As well as his three most well-known masterpieces *A Streetcar Named Desire* (1947), *The Glass Menagerie* (1945) and *Cat on a Hot Tin Roof* (1955), Williams' work comprises further successful plays such as *The Rose Tattoo* (1951), *Camino Real* (1953), *Orpheus Descending (1957), Suddenly Last Summer* (1958), *Sweet Bird of Youth* (1959), *Period of Adjustment* (1960), and *The Night of the Iguana* (1961). His only novel, *The Roman Spring of Mrs Stone* (1950), by contrast, met with a rather negative response.

Vorüberlegungen zum Einsatz des Dramas im Unterricht

Tennessee Williams 1948 veröffentlichtes und im selben Jahr mit dem Pulitzer Prize ausgezeichnetes Drama *A Streetcar Named Desire* bietet neben der Notwendigkeit ausgedehnter Studien des ungeheuer komplexen, facettenhaften und widersprüchlichen Charakters der Protagonistin Blanche Dubois auch die Möglichkeit, eine Vielzahl von Themen, Symbolen sowie Tropen, die eng mit der Grundaussage des Dramas verknüpft sind, näher zu untersuchen. Die hierbei zwangsläufig zur Sprache kommenden Oppositionsmuster Kultur versus Unkultur, Wirklichkeit versus Illusion oder Brutalität versus Dekadenz sowie die hiermit untrennbar verbundenen Spannungen zwischen amerikanischem Süden und Norden ermöglichen nicht nur einen soziologischen bzw. philosophischen Zugriff auf den Dramenstoff, sondern vermögen darüber hinaus auch tiefe und fundierte Einblicke in die amerikanische Geschichte zu geben. Darüber hinaus sollten die für Williams Theaterstücke typische Dramaturgie (detaillierte Bühnenanweisungen, melodramatische Elemente etc.) sowie autobiographische Züge tragende Charakterzeichnungen Anlass dazu gehen, anhand sorgfältig ausgewählter Auszüge Vergleiche mit weiteren von dem Autor verfassten Dramen (z. B. *The Glass Menagerie, Cat on a Hot Tin Roof*) zu ziehen. Dieses Vorgehen scheint nicht nur hinsichtlich der Notwendigkeit einer detaillierten sowie fundierten literaturtheoretischen Analyse des Dramas sinnvoll zu sein, sondern auch im Hinblick auf das überaus wichtige Verständnis der Verbindung zwischen dem Handeln der einzelnen Bühnenfiguren und dem sie umgebenden historischen sowie sozialpolitischen Kontext.

Während die für das Verständnis von Blanches, Stellas und Stanleys sozialem Hintergrund notwendigen Kenntnisse historischer Entwicklungen, die zwischen dem Sezessionskrieg (1861 – 1865) und den 40er-Jahren des 20. Jahrhunderts angesiedelt sind, im Rahmen von sogenannten *pre-reading activities* (Schülerreferate, Auswertung von Dokumentarfilmen etc.) erworben werden können, sollte die Beleuchtung der dem Drama inhärenten Symbolik und Metaphorik sowie die Vornahme intensiver Charakterstudien im Zuge von *while-reading activities* erfolgen. Dieses Vorgehen scheint nicht nur im Hinblick auf die Erreichung des übergeordneten Zieles, ein entdeckendes Lernen unter Einbeziehung heuristischer Methoden zu kultivieren, äußerst sinnvoll zu sein, sondern auch aufgrund der Notwendigkeit eines unablässigen und intensiven *Close Reading,* um Aussagen, Handlungen und Verhaltensweisen der Protagonisten richtig einordnen zu können. Da jedoch nicht alle Sichtweisen und Beweggründe der Protagonisten eindeutig und unzweifelhaft durch die ausschließliche Analyse von Bühnenanweisungen bzw. Dialogen erklärt werden können, bieten sich im Verlaufe der unterrichtlichen Aufarbeitung des Dramas *A Streetcar Named Desire* folglich mannigfaltige Möglichkeiten, im Rahmen der Bearbeitung von Kreativaufgaben Spekulationen über verborgene Motive und Intentionen der Figuren anzustellen.

Die mit dem Handeln der Figuren Blanche, Stanley und Stella in engem Zusammenhang stehende Kernaussage von Williams Drama soll schließlich in Form von *post-reading activities* kritisch beleuchtet werden. Somit wird zum Abschluss der Dramendiskussion nicht nur ein profundes Verständnis der Funktion der einzelnen Figuren herbeigeführt, sondern es wird darüber hinaus auch die Möglichkeit einer fruchtbaren Diskussion hinsichtlich der Sympathielenkung innerhalb des Dramas *A Streetcar Named Desire* eröffnet. Letzterer Aspekt wird insbesondere vor dem Hintergrund der Analyse von Elia Kazans gleichnamigem Film einer genaueren Betrachtung unterzogen.

Abschließend bleibt zu bemerken, dass die Lektüre des Dramas sowohl im Leistungskurs als auch im Grundkurs der gymnasialen Oberstufe erfolgen kann. Während die transparente

Struktur und Handlungsführung des Dramas sowie die Verfügbarkeit einer sehr schüler-freundlichen, reichhaltig annotierten, bei Reclam erschienenen Dramenausgabe (Grundlage des vorliegenden Unterrichtsmodells) für eine Lektüre im Grundkurs sprechen, bieten die Komplexität des Charakters der Protagonistin Blanche sowie die zahlreichen soziologischen sowie historischen Implikationen des Dramas vielfältige Möglichkeiten bzw. Ansätze für eine vertiefende Besprechung im Leistungskurs.

In Nordrhein-Westfalen ist die Lektüre von *A Streetcar Named Desire* bei der Vorbereitung auf das Zentralabitur 2009 obligatorisch.

Klausuren

Im Folgenden werden zwei auf das Drama *A Streetcar Named Desire* bezogene Klausurenvorschläge vorgestellt.

Klausur 1 basiert auf Auszügen, die der ersten Szene des von Tennessee Williams verfassten Dramas *The Glass Menagerie* (1. Szene, S. 21 – 25) entnommen sind und gewährt den Schülerinnen und Schülern nicht nur einen Einblick in die Wertvorstellungen, Sehnsüchte und Hoffnungen der Amanda Wingfield, einer der Protagonistinnen des Dramas, sondern konfrontiert sie darüber hinaus auch mit dem Bild, welches Amandas Sohn Tom von seiner Mutter hat. Um die vielfältigen offenen sowie versteckten Parallelen, welche die Figuren Amanda Wingfield und Blanche DuBois aufweisen, umfassend und präzise analysieren zu können, sollte der Klausur eine vollständige Besprechung des Dramas vorangegangen sein. Dies ist im Übrigen auch angesichts der von den Schülerinnen und Schülern zu bewerkstelligenden Verifizierung bzw. Falsifizierung der Aussagen, welche Tom über seine Mutter und somit indirekt über Blanche trifft, von zentraler Wichtigkeit. In Anbetracht der Tatsache, dass sich der die vorliegenden Auszüge prägende Sprachgebrauch durch eine relativ geringe Komplexität auszeichnet und im Hinblick auf die augenfälligen Gemeinsamkeiten, die Blanche und Amanda aufweisen, kann die Klausur auch in einem Grundkurs gestellt werden.

Klausur 2, welche auf Auszügen aus John Osbornes Drama *Look Back in Anger* (1. Akt, S. 18 – 20) basiert, vermittelt den Schülerinnen und Schülern Einblicke in das Wirken und Handeln von Jimmy, dem tyrannischen, jähzornigen und zynischen Protagonisten des Dramas. Da der Schwerpunkt der Klausur auf der Analyse von Unterschieden bzw. Gemeinsamkeiten zwischen Jimmy und Stanley Kowalski liegt, sollte Williams Drama *A Streetcar Named Desire* bis einschließlich Szene 8 behandelt worden sein. Angesichts der Tatsache, dass Stanleys Verhalten und Sprachgebrauch, insbesondere in Szene 3 und Szene 8, neben vielen offensichtlichen Gemeinsamkeiten auch sehr subtile Unterschiede zu Jimmys Gebaren in dem vorliegenden Auszug aufweist, könnte die Klausur unter der Maßgabe unterschiedlicher Schwerpunktsetzungen sowohl in einem Grundkurs als auch einem Leistungskurs gestellt werden.

Excerpt from Tennessee Williams, *The Glass Menagerie* (scene 1, pp. 21–25)

Amanda Wingfield, a middle-aged woman is having a conversation with her son Tom and her crippled daughter Laura. They are gathered in the living room of Amanda's apartment.
[…]

Laura *(sitting down)*: I'm not expecting any gentlemen callers.

Amanda *(crossing out to the kitchenette, airily)*: Sometimes they come when they are least expected! Why, I remember one Sunday afternoon in Blue Mountain – *(she enters the kitchenette.)*

5 Tom: I know what's coming!

Laura: Yes. But let her tell it.

Tom: Again?

Laura: She loves to tell it. *(Amanda returns with a bowl of dessert).*

Amanda: One Sunday afternoon in Blue Mountain – your mother received – *seventeen!*
10 – gentlemen callers! Why, sometimes there weren't chairs enough to accommodate them all. We had to send the nigger over to bring in folding chairs from the parish house.

Tom *(remaining at the portieres)*: How did you entertain those gentlemen callers?

Amanda: I understood the art of conversation.

15 Tom: I bet you could talk.

Amanda: Girls in those days *knew* how to talk, I can tell you.

Tom: Yes? […]

Amanda: They knew how to entertain their gentlemen callers. It wasn't enough for a girl to be possessed of a pretty face and a graceful figure – although I wasn't slighted in
20 either respect. She also needed to have a nimble wit and a tongue to meet all occasions.

Tom: What did you talk about?

Amanda: Things of importance going on in the world! Never anything coarse or common or vulgar. *(She addresses Tom as though he were seated in the vacant chair at the table*
25 *though he remains by the portieres. He plays this scene as though reading from a script.)* My callers were gentlemen – all! Among my callers were some of the most prominent young planters of the Mississippi Delta – planters and sons of planters! […] There was young Champ Laughlin who later became vice-president of the Delta Planters Bank. Hadley Stevenson who was drowned in Moon Lake and left his widow one hundred and fifty
30 thousand in Government bonds. There were the Cutrere brothers, Wesley and Bates. Bates was one of my bright particular beaux! He got in a quarrel with that wild Wainwright boy. They shot it out on the floor of Moon Lake Casino. Bates was shot through the stomach. Died in the ambulance on his way to Memphis. His widow was also well provided-for, came into eight or ten thousand acres, that's all. She married him on the
35 rebound – never loved her – carried my picture on him the night he died! And there was that boy that every girl in the Delta had set her cap for! That beautiful, brilliant young Fitzhugh boy from Greene County!

Tom: What did he leave his widow?

AMANDA: He never married! Gracious, you talk as though all of my old admirers had
40 turned up their toes to the daisies!

TOM: Isn't this the first you've mentioned that still survives?

AMANDA: That Fitzhugh boy went North and made a fortune – came to be known as the Wolf of Wall Street! [...] whatever he touched turned to gold! And I could have been Mrs. Duncan J. Fitzhugh, mind you! But – I picked your *father*!

45 LAURA *(rising)*: Mother let me clear the table.

AMANDA: No, dear, you go in front and study your typewriter chart. Or practice your shorthand a little. Stay fresh and pretty! – It's almost time for our gentlemen callers to start arriving. *(She flounces girlishly toward the kitchenette.)* How many do you suppose we're going to entertain this afternoon? *(Tom throws down the paper and jumps up with*
50 *a groan.)*

LAURA *(alone in the dining room)*: I don't believe we're going to receive any, mother.

AMANDA *(reappearing airily)*: What? No one – not one? You must be joking! *(Laura nervously echoes her laugh)* [...] Not one gentleman caller? It can't be true there must be a flood, there must have been a tornado!

55 LAURA: It isn't a flood, it's not a tornado, Mother. I'm just not popular like you in Blue Mountain ... *(Tom utters another groan)*

Tennessee Williams: The Glass Menagerie, Stuttgart, Reclam 2000, pp. 21–25

Assignments

1. Outline the course of the conversation in the given excerpt.

2. Compare Amanda Wingfield to Blanche DuBois. What do the two women have in common and what distinguishes them? Pay special attention to their background and their values.

3. "A little woman of great but confused vitality clinging frantically to another time and place. Her characterization must be carefully created, not copied from type. She is not paranoiac, but her life is paranoia. There is much to admire in Amanda, and as much to love and pity as there is to laugh at. Certainly she has endurance and a kind of heroism, and though her foolishness makes her unwittingly cruel at times, there is tenderness in her slight person."
   Comment on the preceding description that Tom gives of his mother and explain why some of the characteristics he attributes to Amanda can also be attributed to Blanche.

Alternative assignment

Recreation of text: After Blanche has been committed to a mental hospital, one of the doctors who works in the hospital asks Stella to give him some information about her sister. Write a dialogue. Pay special attention to the reasons for Blanche's committal to a mental hospital.

Erwartungshorizont zu Klausur 1

zu 1: The starting point for the conversation at hand is Amanda's desire to tell her children Tom and Laura about her experiences of entertaining young gentlemen. Tom, who is apparently able to anticipate the topic of his mother's impending account, seems to be very reluctant to listen to her. His sister Laura, however, manages to persuade him into paying due attention to Amanda's reminiscences. However, as soon as Amanda starts going on and on about her past experiences, Tom sets about asking his mother very straightforward questions that are obviously meant to ridicule Amanda's habit of lecturing her children about the importance of being well-versed in the art of making conversation. Since Tom's questions goad Amanda into providing evidence of her success in that particular area of knowledge, she gives her children detailed accounts of the wealthy and successful men that used to adore her. Although Tom's mocking inquiries about Amanda's apparent disappointment at having married Tom and Laura's father instead of one of her wealthy admirers come close to overtaxing her patience, she is able to curb her temper. Conversely, her eagerness to encourage Laura to improve on her skills at using a typewriter and her overoptimistic view of her daughter's prospects of attracting a lot of eligible young men, finally provoke frustration and anger in Tom.

zu 2: **Similarities:**
- both women set great store by education and etiquette
- both attach great importance to being adored and admired
- they are nostalgic about the days when they had many suitors
- they detest coarseness and vulgarity
- they have a strong propensity for living in the past and thus run the risk of failing to establish contact with reality
- both have a marked class consciousness (Amanda even goes so far as to label her former servant as "nigger", l. 11)
- both are aware of having made mistakes
- since Amanda's crippled daughter Laura is not very likely to attract the attention of many young men and since Blanche, on the other hand, is not very likely to find shelter and protection in the arms of a wealthy and well-respected man, the life of both women is overshadowed by thwarted ambitions

Differences:
- while Blanche still strives for admiration and respect, Amanda is exclusively preoccupied with her daughter's success and reputation
- in contrast to Blanche, Amanda lives in her own flat
- in contrast to Amanda, Blanche is dependent on her sister, or in her words, on "the kindness of strangers"

zu 3: At first glance, the description that Tom gives of his mother seems to be rather confusing because he intermingles positive characteristics with negative ones. But is it really necessary to take his description with a grain of salt? Taking into account that inconsistencies in people's characters are not a new phenomenon and taking a closer look at Amanda's conversation with her children, it might be assumed that Tom's description probably contains a grain of truth. Subjecting Amanda's statements and utterances to close scrutiny, it becomes apparent that despite her being concerned about her children's future, she also has a strong propensity for inadvertently hurting their feelings. By making them aware that marrying their father might have been the wrong decision and instilling her daughter with a feeling of inferiority by enumerating the vast number of admirers she had in the past, Amanda reveals herself to be rather insensitive and callous. Comparable to Blanche, who cannot restrain herself from showing pretensions of superiority, Amanda seems to be completely incapable of escaping the restraints of her bourgeois upbringing. Due to her insistence on good manners, good looks and a good education, her attitude is strongly affected by remarkably conservative and traditional values. Since Amanda as well as Blanche are also very insistent women who do not allow refusal or opposition they not only run the risk of snubbing those around them, but they also quite often lay themselves open to ridicule. Nevertheless, although their mannerisms and their ridiculous attempts to distract attention from their mature womanhood by assuming an air of girlish light-heartedness make them a laughing stock, they also arouse sympathy in the spectator/reader. It is noticeable that both women are in essence tragic figures who are trying in vain to preserve something that has been irretrievably lost: their youth and the chances and opportunities that were connected with it. Since both Amanda and Blanche try very hard to preserve their dignity in the face of thwarted ambitions and impending disappointments, they have "a kind of heroism". However, since they are in the grip of some very strong but undeclared motives that prevent them from facing up to reality and that make them strive frantically for an unattainable goal, they also have to live lives which have turned into a "paranoia".

zu 4: The conversation held by Stella and the doctor has to satisfy the following requirements:
- Stella has to answer questions concerning her relationship with Blanche
- Stella has to account for Blanche's committal to a mental hospital
- she has to give information about her marriage with Stanley
- during the conversation it has to become apparent that she has a guilty conscience and that she is struggling with an inner conflict

Excerpt from: John Osborne, *Look Back in Anger* (Act I, pp. 18–20)

Jimmy Porter, a 25-year-old ex undergraduate who runs a sweet stall, his upper-class wife Alison and his uneducated friend Cliff are gathered in the living room of the Porters' flat.

JIMMY: Do you have to make all that racket?

CLIFF: Oh, sorry.

JIMMY: It's quite a simple thing, you know – turning over a page. Anyway, that's my paper. *(snatches it away)*

5 CLIFF: Oh, don't be so mean!

JIMMY: Price ninepence, obtainable from any newsagent's. Now let me hear the music, for God's sake. [...] *(to Alison)* Are you going to be much longer doing that?

ALISON: Why?

JIMMY: Perhaps you haven't noticed it, but it's interfering with the radio.

10 ALISON: I'm sorry. I shan't be much longer.

A pause. The iron mingles with the music. Cliff shifts restlessly in his chair. Jimmy watches Alison, his foot beginning to twitch dangerously. Presently, he gets up quickly, crossing below Alison to the radio, and turns it off.
What did you do that for?

15 JIMMY: I wanted to listen to the concert, that's all.

ALISON: Well, what's stopping you?

JIMMY: Everyone's making such a din – that's what's stopping me.

ALISON: Well, I'm not sorry, but I can't just stop everything because you want to listen to music.

20 JIMMY: Why not?

ALISON: Really, Jimmy, you're like a child.

JIMMY: Don't try and patronize me. *(turning to Cliff)* She's so clumsy. I watch for her to do the same things every night. The way she jumps on the bed, as if she were stamping on someone's face, and draws the curtains back with a great clatter, in that casually 25 destructive way of hers. It's like someone launching a battleship. Have you ever noticed how noisy women are? [...] Have you? The way they kick the floor about, simply walking over it? Or have you watched them sitting at their dressing tables, dropping their weapons and banging down their bits of boxes and brushes and lipsticks?

He faces her dressing table.

30 I've watched her doing it night after night. When you see a woman in front of her bedroom mirror, you realize what refined form of a butcher she is. [...] Did you ever see some dirty old Arab, sticking his fingers into some mess of lamb fat and gristle? Well, she's just like that. Thank God they don't have many women surgeons! Those primitive hands would have your guts out in no time. Flip! Out it comes, like the powder out of 35 its box. Flop! Back it goes. Like the powder puff on the table.

CLIFF *(grimacing cheerfully)*: Ugh! Stop it!

JIMMY *(moving upstage)*: She'd drop your guts like hair clips and fluff all over the floor. You've got to be fundamentally insensitive to be as noisy and as clumsy as that. [...]

Church bells start ringing outside.

40 Oh, hell! Now the bloody bells have started! *(He rushes to the window)* Wrap it up, will you? Stop ringing those bells! There's somebody going crazy in here! I don't want to hear them!

ALISON: Stop shouting! *(recovering immediately)* You'll have Miss Drury up here.

JIMMY: I don't give a damn about Miss Drury – that mild old gentlewoman doesn't fool
45 me, even if she takes in you two. She's an old robber. She gets more than enough out of us for this place every week. Anyway, she's probably in church, *(points to the window)* swinging on those bloody bells!

Cliff goes to the window and closes it.

CLIFF: Come on now, be a good boy. I'll take us all out, and we'll have a drink.

John Osborne: Look Back in Anger, London, Faber and Faber 1996, pp. 18–20

Assignments

1. Outline the topic of conversation as well as its development in the given excerpt and explain the behaviour of the people involved in it.

2. Point out what Jimmy and Stanley Kowalski have in common and what distinguishes them. Pay special attention to their behaviour and the language they use.

3. Comment on the following statement: "To Alison and Stella, being married means to suffer humiliation, to be paralyzed with fear and to live in a constant state of anxiety."

Alternative assignment

Recreation of text: Write a letter to Jimmy in which you comment on his attitude as well as his behaviour. Draw on your knowledge of the terrible effect that Stanley Kowalski's behaviour has had on Blanche and Stella.

Erwartungshorizont zu Klausur 2

zu 1: The given extract consists mainly of long tirades of abuse which Jimmy heaps on women, in particular, their lack of sensitivity and consideration. Much of his abuse spills over into scathing, if somewhat bitterly humorous attacks on his wife Alison. Since Jimmy wants to listen to a concert on the radio, he is annoyed about the noise that is being caused by the activities that his friend Cliff and his wife Alison are engaged in: While Alison is ironing, Cliff skims through Jimmy's newspaper. Although Jimmy manages to take away the newspaper from Cliff and despite Alison's assurance that she is about to stop ironing, Jimmy ends up giving vent to his pent-up anger by abruptly switching off the radio. Since Alison then scolds him for being childish, he starts working himself up into an obsessional monologue. It should be noted that he turns to Cliff while condemning Alison and women in general. Thus, it becomes apparent that there is a great deal of antagonism between Jimmy and his wife, an antagonism mitigated by the presence of Cliff who acts as a buffer between them. Jimmy's anger at the ringing of church bells and his violent verbal attacks on Mrs. Dury, the landlady, on the other hand, reveal his hostility towards social institutions and his marked class-consciousness.

zu 2: **Similarities:**
- both are class conscious, hence their scepticism towards the world of the middle/upper classes; it seems that they are obsessed by the fear of being swindled out of their money by members of the more privileged classes
- whenever Jimmy and Stanley have to face refusal or opposition, they tend to fly into a rage; thus both tend to be extremely irritable and hot-tempered
- both are peremptory and domineering; in other words, they tend to boss people about and insist on immediate obedience and submission
- both are very possessive about the things they own (be it newspapers or bottles of whisky)
- both heap abuse on women
- both have the habit of entertaining friends at home
- their friends tend to appease them

Differences:
- in contrast to Stanley, Jimmy is extremely articulate on the subjects he brings up
- although Jimmy as well as Stanley make use of abusive language, Jimmy's ability to talk fluently and draw ironic parallels and comparisons mark him out as more sophisticated than Stanley
- in contrast to Stanley, Jimmy obviously has a propensity for soliloquizing
- compared to the energetic and tough Stanley, Jimmy seems to be rather fastidious and prissy

zu 3: a) arguments in favour of the statement:
- both women are harassed by their respective husbands: while Jimmy merely heaps abuse on Alison, Stanley even goes so far as to beat Stella up
- since both Stanley and Jimmy abuse their wives in the presence of other people, Stella and Alison have to put up with harrowing and humiliating experiences
- although Alison and Stella perform their household chores at regular intervals, their work is not appreciated by their husbands; while Jimmy complains about the noise that is caused by Alison's ironing, Stanley takes it for granted that Stella serves his meals to him

b) arguments against the statement:
- in labelling her husband as childish, Alison makes it clear that she does not take him seriously
- since she levels criticism at her husband's table manners, Stella proves to be more self-confident than frightened
- selling out her sister Blanche for sexual gratification reveals Stella to be extremely attracted to her husband
- although Jimmy insists on immediate obedience, Alison does not stop ironing immediately after he orders to do so
- instead of dreading her husband's violent outbursts, Stella accepts Stanley's behaviour with empathy and understanding
- Alison is not afraid to ask Jimmy to stop shouting

zu 4: The students are expected to concentrate on/level criticism at Jimmy's
- intolerance
- callousness
- hostility towards religion
- lack of appreciation for the chores his wife has to perform
- domineering nature
- irascibility/hot temper
- possessiveness
- propensity for humiliating his wife in the presence of other people

Konzeption des Unterrichts- modells

Das vorliegende Unterrichtsmodell verfolgt das übergeordnete Ziel, Ursachen und Wirkungen der sich in Williams Drama *A Streetcar Named Desire* dramatisch zuspitzenden Interaktionen und Ereignisse vor dem Hintergrund eines unterschwellig schwelenden Kultur- und Klassenkampfes zwischen amerikanischem Norden und amerikanischem Süden zu untersuchen. Da das didaktische Konzept des Unterrichtsmodells darauf ausgerichtet ist, die genaue Analyse einzelner Dramenpassagen der allgemeinen Bewertung von Charakteren, Ereignissen und Entwicklungen voranzustellen, ist es nicht notwendig, dass die Schülerinnen und Schüler das Drama zu Beginn der unterrichtlichen Diskussion komplett gelesen haben. Die Bearbeitung von *pre-reading activities,* die das Ziel verfolgen, den historischen sowie politischen Hintergrund des Dramas aufzuarbeiten, soll den Schülerinnen und Schülern darüber hinaus den Einstieg in die Dramenbesprechung sowie das Verständnis der in dem Drama manifest werdenden Antagonismen erleichtern.

Component 1 beleuchtet schwerpunkthaft das durch die beiden Protagonisten Blanche und Stanley verkörperte Aufeinandertreffen zweier diametral verschiedener Wertesysteme und Weltbilder. Vor dem Hintergrund eines immer noch unterschwellig schwelenden Kulturkampfes zwischen amerikanischem Norden und amerikanischem Süden werden insbesondere die Verhaltensmuster und der Sprachgebrauch der oben erwähnten Protagonisten einer genaueren Betrachtung unterzogen. Die sich hieraus ableitenden und teilweise nur sehr versteckt zum Vorschein kommenden Grundüberzeugungen und Charaktereigenschaften werden im Rahmen verschiedener Arbeits- und Sozialformen analysiert und bewertet.

Component 2 rückt sowohl den immer manifester werdenden Klassenhass zwischen Blanche und Stanley als auch die immer größer werdende Kluft zwischen den Schwestern Blanche und Stella in den Mittelpunkt der Aufmerksamkeit. Die sich aus den oben genannten Entwicklungen ergebenden Konsequenzen für Blanches Verhältnis zu dem etwas steifen Junggesellen Mitch werden zum Anlass genommen, Beweggründe, Hoffnungen und Aussichten der Protagonistin Blanche einer genaueren Analyse zu unterziehen. Die relativ große Fülle von Kreativaufgaben, welche die Schülerinnen und Schüler in diesem Zusammenhang bearbeiten, soll nicht nur eine emotionale Auseinandersetzung ermöglichen, sondern darüber hinaus auch eine Identifikation mit den Wertvorstellungen und der Gedankenwelt Blanches gewährleisten.

Component 3 ist im Wesentlichen darauf ausgerichtet, die Ursachen für die Demütigungen und Verletzungen derer sich die sprichwörtlich immer weiter in die Enge getriebene Blanche ausgesetzt sieht, zu ergründen. Blanches Vergewaltigung durch Stanley, welche letztlich zu ihrer Persönlichkeitszerstörung und Einlieferung in eine Nervenheilanstalt führt, soll schließlich zum Anlass genommen werden, sowohl die Sympathielenkung als auch die Verwendung melodramatischer Elemente in Williams Drama aufzuzeigen und zu untersuchen. Die hierbei zum Tragen kommenden Arbeits- und Sozialformen sind vielfach darauf ausgerichtet, den Schülerinnen und Schülern einen möglichst selbstständigen sowie kreativen Umgang mit den in dem Drama dargestellten Ereignissen zu ermöglichen.

Die in *Component 4* vorgenommene Filmanalyse umfasst neben der Untersuchung diverser Kameraeinstellungen und deren Funktionen eine detaillierte Analyse der Unterschiede, welche Elia Kazans Filmversion zu dem ursprünglichen Drama aufweist. Anhand der Gegenüberstellung von Dramenpassagen und Filmszenen sollen die Schülerinnen und Schüler nicht nur Ursachen und Wirkungen der vorgenommenen Modifikationen analysieren, sondern darüber hinaus auch persönliche Wertungen der zu beobachtenden Abwandlungen vornehmen. Um einen möglichst souveränen und kritischen Umgang mit den in der Filmversion vorgenommenen Änderungen zu ermöglichen, setzen sich die Lernenden im Rahmen diverser Kreativaufgaben mit den unterschiedlichen Sichtweisen der Zensurbehörde MPAA (Motion Picture Association of America) und den Künstlern Tennessee Williams und Elia Kazan auseinander.

Two worlds collide

1.1 The arrival of Blanche at her sister's place

Das Eintreffen der Protagonistin Blanche DuBois am Wohnort (New Orleans, Elysian Fields) ihrer Schwester Stella ist streng genommen von drei separaten Begegnungen geprägt, die sowohl Einblicke in Blanches Gemütszustand bzw. charakterliche Disposition gewähren als auch wichtige Einzelheiten ihres familiären, beruflichen sowie kulturellen Hintergrundes aufdecken. So geben die zwei kurzen Gespräche, welche sie mit Eunice und Stanley führt sowie die sehr intensive Konversation mit ihrer Schwester Stella nicht nur Auskunft darüber, dass es sich bei Blanche um eine aus ehemals begüterten Verhältnissen stammenden Englischlehrerin handelt, die schwer am Verlust ihres Mannes und dem Familienanwesen Belle Reve trägt, sondern es wird darüber hinaus überaus deutlich, mit welch großen Vorbehalten und Ressentiments sie den Lebensverhältnissen bzw. dem sozialen Umfeld ihrer Schwester Blanche gegenübersteht. Während sich ihr Befremden bei ihren Begegnungen mit Stanley und Eunice in großer Reserviertheit und Befangenheit äußert, gibt Blanche in Gegenwart ihrer Schwester Stella in einem Anfall von Hysterie eindeutig zu verstehen, dass sie deren mangelnden Einsatz für die Belange der Familie DuBois sowie die Heirat mit einem Polen als Klassenverrat betrachtet. Stanley als *polack* beschimpfend gibt sie sowohl ihrem Klassenhass als auch ihrer Enttäuschung über den Verlust des Familienanwesens Belle Reve Ausdruck. Blanches Alkoholsucht, die manifest wird als sie in Abwesenheit ihrer Schwester einige gierige Schlucke aus einer Stanley gehörenden Whiskyflasche nimmt, unterstreicht ihre innere Verzweiflung und Zerrissenheit mit großer Nachhaltigkeit.

Um zu gewährleisten, dass die Schülerinnen und Schüler sich nicht nur der großen Verunsicherung und Verletzlichkeit Blanches, welche sich in ihrem fragilen Äußeren, ihrer permanenten Suche nach Bestätigung und nicht zuletzt ihrem Ohnmachtsanfall am Ende der ersten Szene manifestieren, sondern auch der Arroganz bzw. des Snobismus, mit welchem sie auf Eunice und Stanley hinabschaut, bewusst werden, ist es von entscheidender Wichtigkeit, dass sie sowohl die Bühnenanweisungen als auch Blanches Äußerungen einer genauen Beobachtung unterziehen. Somit ergeht zunächst folgender Arbeitsauftrag an die Schülerinnen und Schüler:

> Make a list of the essential pieces of information the stage directions on pages 8–11 give you. Find out what the stage directions reveal about Blanche's character and her attitude.

Die von den Schülerinnen und Schülern hervorgebrachten Ergebnisse könnten in folgendem Tafelbild münden:

Stage directions	Conclusions
arriving at Elysian Fields her facial expression bespeaks "shocked disbelief" (p. 8, l. 25)	→ accustomed to more exclusive residential areas → very sensitive person → class conscious because she apparently considers it to be beneath her sister's dignity to live in Elysian Fields
she is overdressed (pp. 8/9)	→ she is apparently not aware of the conspicuousness of her clothes and the impression they might create
"uncertain manner"/is compared to a "moth" (p. 9, l. 7)	→ like the insect that mainly flies toward and is attracted to the dangerous light Blanche is placed in a dilemma: although needing the protection of the night (concealment of weak spots), she cannot resist the lure of glamour and attention
not believing that her sister lives in a place like Elysian Fields, she is close to becoming hysterical (p. 9, l. 10)	→ she lacks patience and composure
she is not able to come to terms with the shabbiness and messiness of her sister's flat (p. 11, l. 1)	→ she is very fastidious
she does not try to hide her annoyance at Eunice's curiosity/inquisitiveness (p. 11, l. 10 ff.)	→ she does not respects her sister's acquaintances

Da die bisher von den Schülerinnen und Schülern gezogenen Schlussfolgerungen allesamt auf Bühnenanweisungen basieren, sollte in einem nächsten Unterrichtsschritt überprüft werden, inwieweit Blanches Äußerungen gegenüber Eunice zur Erweiterung ihres Charakterbildes dienen. Zu diesem Zweck lesen die Schülerinnen und Schüler die von Blanche gemachten Äußerungen unter folgender Fragestellung:

> **What strikes you about Blanche's mode of expression when talking to Eunice and what does it reveal about her attitude towards her new surroundings?**

Die Präsentation der Ergebnisse im Plenum könnte über Folie erfolgen:

Blanche's mode of expression	Example	Conclusion
Her utterances are strikingly short.	On p. 11 she answers Eunice's questions using just the single word "yes" four times	She is reserved and evasive.
Several questions she asks are rhetorical questions.	"This – can this be her home?" (p. 10, l. 2)	She does not expect anybody to answer her question → Indication of her self-absorption and bewilderment.
She makes no bones about raising objections against Eunice's proposals.	"How could I – do that?" (p. 10, l. 20)	She resents being treated with the casual familiarity of an equal.

Weitere charakterliche Eigenheiten Blanches, welche im Verlauf ihrer Unterhaltungen mit Stella und Stanley sowie während der kurzen Phase ihres Alleinseins in der schwesterlichen Wohnung manifest werden, sollten die Schülerinnen und Schüler in Form von arbeitsteiligen Gruppenarbeiten aufdecken. Dieses Vorgehen erweist sich nicht nur aufgrund der Tatsache, dass der komplexe und nuancenreiche verbale Austausch, der zwischen Blanche und Stella bzw. Blanche und Stanley vonstattengeht, mit einem besonders hohen Maß an Konzentration betrachtet werden muss, sondern auch aufgrund der sich bietenden Möglichkeit, einen lebhaften Informationsaustausch zwischen den mit verschiedenen Arbeitsaufträgen betrauten Gruppen zu initiieren, als besonders sinnvoll.

Somit ergehen folgende Arbeitsaufträge an die Schülerinnen und Schüler:

Group 1, read p. 13– p. 24 (l. 7) and work on the following tasks:

a) Make up a diagram that illustrates the various phases of the conversation between Blanche and Stella and describes the sisters' behaviour.
b) Draw up a list of adjectives that can be used to pinpoint the sisters' demeanour.
c) Inform your classmates about the conclusions that you have drawn concerning the sisters' relationship.

Tasks a) and b) should be presented on a transparency.

Group 2, work on the following tasks:

a) Point out what Blanche's utterances and the stage direction on p. 12 reveal.
b) Before reading Blanche's and Stan's conversation on pp. 26–28, carefully read through Stanley's first appearance on pp. 7–8 and note down what you expect the conversation to be like. Give reasons for your assumptions.
c) Perform Blanche and Stanley's first conversation in front of your classmates and pay close attention to the stage directions by making extensive use of mime and gestures.

Die von Gruppe 1 erarbeiteten Ergebnisse könnten folgende Form annehmen:

zu a):

phase	topic of conversation	Blanche's behaviour	Stella's behaviour
1. welcome p. 13 – p. 14 (l. 8)	there is no actual topic of conversation because Stella hardly has a chance to utter a word	she monopolizes the conversation and makes a series of remarks that refer to her state of mind, her opinion about Stella's flat and her fear of glaring light; more-over, she is eager to have a drink	she merely reacts to Blanche's torrent of words and comments quite ironically on her sister's verbosity
2. p. 14 (l. 8) – p. 15 (l. 14)	Stella's poor living condi-tions	she does not recoil from expressing her horror and disgust about her sister's flat	Stella tries to convince Blanche of the adequacy of her living conditions
3. p. 15 (l. 15) – p. 16 (l. 6)	Stella's calm and com-posure; Blanche's looks and her job at the school	Blanche lays bare her loneliness and criticizes Stella's reticence and lack of inquisitiveness; she wants her sister to comment on her looks, and what is more, to inquire about her job	Stella points out quite tentatively that she has little chance "saying much"; it becomes apparent that she intends to make her sister feel at ease and that she by no means wants to hurt her by being rash
4. p. 16 (l. 17) – p. 17 (l. 9)	Stella and Blanche's looks	although Blanche comments quite bluntly on her sister's looks and advises her to change her hairstyle, she expects Stella to pay her compli-ments	although Blanche's fussiness about clothes, hairstyles and weight apparently puts a strain on Stella, she does what her sister expects her to do: she compliments Blanche on her good looks
5. p. 18 (l. 10) – p. 21 (l. 9)	the facilities in Blanche's flat, Stella's husband Stanley	Blanche inquires about Stella's husband Stanley, being anxious that Stanley might not like or accept her, she starts bombarding Stella with a lot of questions about him	Stella gives details about Stanley's background, his friends and her feelings towards him; although it becomes apparent that she is madly in love with Stanley, she is aware of the unbridgeable cultural differences between him and her sister
6. p. 21 (l. 10) – p. 24 (l. 7)	the loss of the family mansion Belle Reve	in a long speech, full of the unspoken (but strongly hinted at) horrors of her life at Belle Reve she speaks of her own suffering and of her sister's selfish indiffe-rence; Blanche's outburst is accusatory and wounding, and is meant to be so	Stella tries to extract the plain facts concerning the loss of Belle Reve from her sister; deeply hurt by her sister's innuendos and recriminations, she finally bursts into tears

Adjectives that indicate the quality of Blanche's demeanour:
hot-tempered, rash, blunt, over-excited, inquisitive, hysterical, aggressive
Adjectives that indicate the quality of Stella's demeanour:
patient, sober, calm, understanding, compliant

zu b): Conclusions that can be drawn concerning the relationship between Stella and Blanche:

Although Blanche teases, criticizes and even accuses her sister Stella in the course of their conversation, it would not be accurate to claim that the sisters' relationship is strained. On the contrary, Blanche's worries about the poor conditions Stella is living in, her use of terms of endearment ("Stella for star") and her favourable, if somewhat ironic, comments on her sister's looks and behaviour, reveal her to be utterly fond of Stella. By saying "You're all I've got in the world ..." and thus running the risk of laying herself open to ridicule, Blanche intimates that she not only loves her sister, but that she also places unconditional trust in Stella's loyalty and support.

As for Stella, it is apparent that she is tolerant of her sister's propensity for monopolizing conversations, changing topics of conversation at will, complaining, criticizing and ranting. Thus, in putting up with her sister's fussiness and the conniving implicit in her violent outbursts, Stella gives the impression of being a patient and experienced psychiatrist dealing with the familiar idiosyncrasies of a well-known patient. Stella's outrage at her sister's attempt at denigrating Stanley, on the other hand, is a first indication of her unwillingness to put up with insults levelled at her husband. Thus, it remains to he seen whether Stella's display of tolerance and patience is based on love, affection, consideration or merely on necessity.

Die von Gruppe 2 erarbeiteten Ergebnisse könnten folgende Form annehmen:

zu 1: It is obvious that Blanche has become hooked on alcohol and is very eager to keep her addiction beneath the surface.

zu 2: Before reading the conversation between Stanley and Blanche, we thought that their first encounter might be characterized by a strained atmosphere because:
- in contrast to Stanley, Blanche is very prissy and refined
- Blanche is prejudiced against her sister's surroundings and acquaintances
- Stanley might take offence at/make fun of Blanche's priggishness, etc.
- Stanley's crude language and coarse manners might repel Blanche

zu 3: The students' performance in front of their classmates is supposed to emphasize not only Stanley's dominance and Blanche's defensiveness, but also the cultural as well as educational gap between them. By paying close attention to the stage directions, the students should be able to bring out the slyness, machismo and inability to be swayed that are suggested by Stanley's appraisal of Blanche and his inquiries about her job and marriage.

Um einen möglichst umfangreichen verbalen Austausch innerhalb der Lerngruppe zu gewährleisten, sind die Schülerinnen und Schüler gefordert, die Darbietungen ihrer Kurskameraden unter folgenden Aufgabenstellungen zu kommentieren bzw. zu analysieren:

> Group 2, comment on the conclusions that have been drawn by group 1. Group 1, what does your classmates' performance tell you about the conversation held by Blanche and Stanley and to what extent do their speculations about their first talk correspond to the actual course of the conversation.

Um die Schülerinnen und Schüler in die Lage zu versetzen, die vielfältigen Informationen und Andeutungen hinsichtlich Blanches Vergangenheit und die sich hieraus möglicherweise ergebenden Konflikte mit ihrer Schwester und deren Ehemann treffend einordnen zu können, werden sie abschließend dazu aufgefordert, einen adäquaten Titel bzw. Aufhänger für Szene 1 zu finden. Da jedoch allein die Wahl eines Titels oder Aufhängers die Lerngruppe voraussichtlich nicht zu einer hinreichenden Reflexion über den Enthüllungscharakter und die Dimension von Szene 1 zu bewegen vermag, sollte in jedem Fall auf einer Begründung für die von Schülerseite unterbreiteten Vorschläge bestanden werden. Ein angemessener Arbeitsauftrag sowie eine hierauf bezogene Schüleräußerung könnten wie folgt lauten:

> Find a suitable title or slogan that epitomizes the incidents and implications of scene 1.
> Give reasons for your choice/your suggestions.
>
> Choice of title: Two worlds collide
>
> Reason for choice: In scene 1, it becomes apparent that Blanche's sensitivity and fastidiousness are incompatible with Stanley's coarseness and pragmatism. Clashes between the two protagonists seem to be imminent.

Mit der Zielsetzung, eine Bewertung der von den Schülerinnen und Schülern dargebrachten Vorschlägen vorzunehmen, sollten diese an der Tafel oder auf einer Folie gesammelt werden und im Anschluss unter folgender Aufgabenstellung im Plenum diskutiert werden:

> Subject your classmates' suggestions to close scrutiny and comment on their suitability.

In Anbetracht der Tatsache, dass die Schülerinnen und Schüler im Rahmen der Bearbeitung der vorangegangenen Aufgabenstellungen zwar schon einen klaren Eindruck von Stanleys Rohheit und übersteigertem Selbstbewusstsein gewonnen haben, jedoch möglicherweise noch keine klare Vorstellung von seiner Lebensphilosophie bzw. von dem in seinen Äußerungen durchschimmernden Argwohn und Machismo entwickelt haben, sollten sie im Rahmen einer Hausaufgabe Stanleys Sprachgebrauch sowie die seine Persönlichkeit umreißenden Bühnenanweisungen einer genauen Untersuchung unterziehen. Diese Art des Vorgehens versetzt die Schülerinnen und Schüler nicht nur in die Lage, die Funktion und Ausprägung der Figur Stanley genauer einordnen zu können, sondern sie ermöglicht darüber hinaus einen adäquaten Einstieg in die Diskussion des sich in Szene 2 deutlich abzeichnenden Antagonismus zwischen Blanche und Stanley. Somit bearbeiten die Schülerinnen und Schüler in Form einer Hausaufgabe ein mit Beschreibungen sowie Aussagen Stanleys gespicktes Arbeitsblatt (Copy 1) unter folgender Aufgabenstellung:

> What do the following descriptions and statements tell us about Stanley's personality and his function in the play?

Stanley

I. Descriptions (stage directions) in scene 1

1. "… twenty-eight or thirty years old, roughly dressed in blue denim work clothes. Stanley carries his bowling jacket and a red-stained package from the butcher's." (p. 7, ll. 10–13)

   The impression that is conveyed by Stanley: _____

   _____

   _____

   _____

   His function in the play: _____

   _____

   _____

   _____

   _____

2. "He heaves the package at her (Stella). She cries out in protest but manages to catch it: then she laughs breathlessly. Her husband and his companion have already started back around the corner." (p. 8, ll. 4–7)

   The impression that is conveyed by Stanley: _____

   _____

   _____

   _____

   His function in the play: _____

   _____

   _____

   _____

3. "He is of medium height, about five feet eight or nine, and strongly, compactly built. Animal joy in his being is implicit in all his movements and attitudes. Since earliest manhood the centre of his life has been pleasure with women, the giving and taking of it, not with weak indulgence, dependently, but with the power and pride of a richly feathered male bird among hens. Branching out from this complete and satisfying centre are all the auxiliary channels of his life, such as his heartiness with men, his appreciation of rough humour, his love of good drink and food and games, his car, his radio, everything that is his, that bears his emblem of the gaudy seed-bearer. He sizes women up at a glance, with sexual classifications, crude images flashing into his mind and determining the way he smiles at them." (p. 25, ll. 8–20–p. 26, ll. 1–3)

   The impression he conveys: _____

   _____

His function in the play: _____

_____

_____

II. Statements

1. "H'lo. Where's the little woman (Stella)?" (p. 26, l. 8)

   Conclusions that can be drawn from the statement: _____

   _____

   _____

   _____

   _____

   _____

2. "Liquor goes fast in hot weather." […] "Some people rarely touch it, but it touches them very often."
   (p. 26, ll. 17–18 and ll. 21–22)

   Conclusions that can be drawn from the statement: _____

   _____

   _____

   _____

   _____

3. "I never was a very good English student. How long you here for, Blanche?" (p. 27, ll. 12–13)

   Conclusions that can be drawn from the statement: _____

   _____

   _____

   _____

   _____

4. "I'm afraid I'll strike you as being the unrefined type. Stella's spoke of you a good deal. You were married once, weren't you?" (p. 27, ll. 27–29)

   Conclusions that can be drawn from the statement: _____

   _____

   _____

   _____

   _____

1.2 Suspicion, smugness and sheepishness

Da die sich in Szene 2 immer deutlicher manifestierende Kluft zwischen Stanley und Blanche nicht nur auf einem Antagonismus der Geschlechter beruht, sondern darüber hinaus auch klare Bezüge zu einem Antagonismus der innerhalb der amerikanischen Gesellschaft existierenden Klassen aufzeigt, sollte der ausführlichen Besprechung der Hausaufgabe (siehe 1.1) die Präsentation eines im Vorfeld der Unterrichtseinheit verteilten Schülerreferats vorangehen, welches die politischen bzw. gesellschaftlichen Entwicklungen in den USA zwischen 1800 und 1940 aufarbeitet. Da der Fabrikarbeiter Stanley Kowalski bedingt durch seinen Pragmatismus und seine Agilität im Gegensatz zu der dekadenten und lebensuntüchtigen Südstaatlerin Blanche als Repräsentant einer Einwandergeneration zu sehen ist, die sich den Idealen des durch Industrialisierung und Innovation geprägten amerikanischen Nordens verschrieben hat, sollte das Schülerreferat sowohl die widerstreitenden Interessen des Nordens und Südens als auch die hiermit eng verknüpfte unterschiedliche Einstellung gegenüber fremden Rassen bzw. Nationalitäten, welche den beiden Landesteilen eigen ist, thematisiert werden.

Die Ereignisse, Entwicklungen und Eckdaten auf *Copy 2* sollten in dem Schülerreferat Erwähnung finden.

Die im Anschluss an das Schülerreferat vonstattengehende Präsentation der Hausaufgabe *(Copy 1)* könnte zu folgenden Ergebnissen geführt haben:

I.1: <u>The impression that Stanley conveys:</u>
Due to the description of Stanley's clothes, the reader sees at a glance that he probably belongs to the working class. Paying attention to the adverb "roughly" and the adjective "red-stained" that Williams uses in order to describe Stanley's outward appearance and the package of meat he carries, it also becomes apparent that Stanley, right from the beginning, is surrounded by an aura of toughness and savage masculinity. He literally represents life in the raw.
<u>Stanley's function:</u>
Stanley's carrying a "red-stained package from the butcher's" and a "bowling jacket" reveal him to be the ordinary, lower-class breadwinner who devotes himself to typically virile pursuits. In addition, it should be noted that the coarseness of his clothes is in sharp contrast to Blanche's strikingly feminine and elegant apparel. Thus, Stanley quite noticeably functions as Blanche's antagonist.

I.2: <u>The impression Stanley conveys:</u>
Not taking the trouble to put the package of meat into his wife's hands in a decent manner and turning his back on her immediately after having arrived at his place seem to be indications of Stanley's tendency to treat his wife with a lack of respect.
<u>Stanley's function:</u>
Stanley proves to be the embodiment of the hard and insensitive macho man.

I.3: <u>The impression Stanley conveys:</u>
Stanley's strong and exclusive attachment to the physical world (sexuality, drink, food) mark him as rather primitive and uneducated. Since beauty and sex-appeal are apparently the only criteria he lays down for the appraisal of women, he also proves to be chauvinistic. Being compared to a "male bird" even intensifies the aura of male arrogance and machismo that surrounds him from the very beginning of the drama.

A chronology

Important incidents and developments that have had a great impact on relations between the American North and the American South:

1800–1829	<u>Slavery</u> becomes the distinctive badge that demarcates two rival regions: The American North and the American South
1820s	The Northern States start <u>industrializing</u> and become far more urbanized than the South. Consequently, they are more likely to attract immigrants who give them a far greater <u>ethnic und social diversity</u>.
1825	Economic divisions lead to political conflict. Anxious to promote domestic manufacturers, the Northern States generally favour <u>high tariffs</u> to deter foreign, and especially British, industrial imports. This is anathema to the Southern cotton lords, who depend on British mills as their chief market and benefit from the importation of cheap food and finished goods.
1830s	A new radical movement (**the abolitionists**) arises following the recognition that the <u>slave system</u> is not going to simply vanish of its own accord.
1830	Portentous public debate between Northern Senator Daniel Webster and South Carolina Senator Robert Y. Hayne, the latter warning that the "<u>American system</u>" is part of a <u>war against the South</u>.
1831	<u>William Lloyd Garrison</u> founds the newspaper **_The Liberator_** with heavy support from free blacks.
1832	Vice President John C. Calhoun advocates the extreme <u>states' rights doctrine</u> that individual states can nullify laws they deem unconstitutional, and South Carolina quickly puts this into practice by refusing to enforce the new tariff.
1839	Theodore Dwight Weld and Angelina Grimke publish the book _Slavery As It Is_, which catalogues for a Northern audience the worst horrors of the system.
1830s/1840s	<u>**Abolitionism**</u> is a nightmare for Southerners for whom slavery has become a source of profit as well as a symbolic badge that differentiates them from the <u>vulgar masses of the North</u>. Consequently, <u>anti-black sentiment</u> is not only rife in communities with a Southern population, but also in Northern regions that are economically tied to the South or who resent former slaves settling in free communities in Northern cities.
1850s	Northern jurisdiction assists the South in the <u>recapture of fleeing slaves</u>.
1852	Harriet Beecher Stove's novel _Uncle Tom's Cabin_ is published. The novel depicts the brutalities of slavery.

1855	Senator Stephen A. Douglas's **Kansas-Nebraska Act** resolves that, in these two states, the slavery issue can be resolved by popular sovereignty. Settlers supporting both opinions begin adamantly claiming their lands, und the ensuing conflicts constitute a virtual <u>civil war</u>. Atrocities are common.
1856	The Kansas-Nebraska Act provokes antislavery militants to desert the existing parties (Whigs, Democrats) to form a new grouping which becomes the <u>Republican Party</u>. In the process, the <u>Whigs cease to exist</u>.
1857	The Supreme Court rules that fleeing slaves are so-called <u>noncitizens</u> who have no right to sue in court. Blacks as a whole are dismissed as a degraded race, with no inherent rights beyond what whites choose to grant.
1860	At a Democratic Party convention, the extremist John C. Breckinridge is chosen as presidential candidate. The process of disunion begins with the <u>secession of South Carolina</u> in December.
1861	<u>Abraham Lincoln</u>, who has declared himself implacably opposed to "the social and political equality of the white and black races" becomes president. By the start of February, six more states have seceded, including Florida, Georgia, Alabama, Mississippi, Louisiana and Texas. The rebellious government forms a new **Confederate States of America**, complete with its own president, <u>Jefferson Davis</u>. In April, Confederate troops fire upon the flag at Fort Sunter in Charleston harbour. Within days, Lincoln calls for troops und orders a blockade of the South. From this point on, the country is at war.
1861–65	**<u>Civil War</u>**
1865	On 9 April, <u>Robert E. Lee</u>, the most important Confederate Commander, <u>surrenders</u> to <u>Ulysses S. Grant</u>, the commander of the Federal Forces at Appomattox courthouse in Virginia. By the middle of May, all Confederate resistance has ended. On 14 April, <u>Abraham Lincoln is assassinated</u> by Confederate agents.

<u>Far-reaching consequences of the war:</u>
- Southern suspicion of Northern "carpetbaggers" (immigrants from the North) and Southern scalawags (traitors) is stirred up by the Ku Klux Klan, which flourishes into the early 1940s.
- Even today, hate and discrimination against blacks is endemic in some Southern regions.

Stanley's function:
See I.1 and I.2

II.1: <u>Conclusions that can be drawn from the statement:</u>
Although calling Stella "little woman" is by no means meant to be an insult or an offensive remark, the adjective "little" might indicate that Stanley feels superior to his wife. Furthermore, the use of the generic term "woman" instead of her first name Stella, probably hints at his subconscious impression that his wife is not an individual but merely someone who fulfils a particular function.

II.2: <u>Conclusions that can be drawn from the statement:</u>
Stanley's comments on the consumption of alcohol turn out to be surprisingly perceptive and witty. By making use of the chiasmus "Some people rarely touch it, but it touches them often", he not only proves to be well-versed in the art of rhetoric, but also gives the impression of having a hunch that Blanche's defensiveness has something to do with her alcohol problems. Nevertheless, whether punning on the consumption of alcohol is a clear indication of his perceptiveness or mere intuition remains to be seen.

II. 3: <u>Conclusions that can be drawn from the statement:</u>
In informing Blanche about his lack of talent for the English language and providing evidence for this lack by asking a question that is wrong according to the rules of grammar ("How long you here for, Blanche"), Stanley seems to want to make it obvious that he is not interested in creating a favourable impression. It is, however, not clear if Stanley's rapid change of the topic of conversation is a deliberate and subtle manoeuvre to show Blanche his contempt for her job or whether he has simply lost interest in talking about the English language. Ironically, Stanley's non-grammatical speech is in sharp contrast to the partly sophisticated language he uses in the preceding part of his conversation with Blanche (see p. 26).

II.4: <u>Conclusions that can be drawn from the statement:</u>
Stanley's assumption that Blanche might regard him as "unrefined" shows that he is aware of the class antagonism between himself and his wife's sister. Comparable to the part of the conversation in which he admits to lacking talent for the English language, he further confirms his assumption by posing a question that is in indeed "unrefined". However, it is not definitely clear if his inquiring about Blanche's marriage and thus opening old wounds is a cynical attempt to expose one of her weak spots. Since their conversation can be subsumed under the category of small talk, it cannot be ruled out that Stanley's inquiry about Blanche's marriage might have quite arbitrarily popped into his head.

Stanleys Verdacht hinsichtlich betrügerischer Absichten Blanches wird in Szene 2 sowohl von dieser selbst als auch von Stella ad absurdum geführt. Die sich vor diesem Hintergrund entspinnende vielschichtige, nuancenreiche, hitzig aufgeladene und somit tiefe Einblicke in die Persönlichkeitsstruktur der beteiligten Charaktere zulassende verbale Interaktion sollte im Zuge der Besprechung von Szene 2 einer ausgedehnten Untersuchung unterzogen werden. Besonders intensiv sollten hierbei die Argumentationslinien bzw. der Habitus der Protagonisten Blanche, Stanley und Stella beleuchtet werden. Zur Erreichung dieses Zieles wird

Stanley's suspicions and Stella's excuses

Stanley

The suspicions Blanche arouses in him: _____

_____

_____

_____

Reasons for his suspicions:

_____

_____

_____

_____

_____

_____

The way he shows his suspicions:

_____

_____

_____

_____

_____

_____

Stella

The way she tries to dispel Stanley's doubts about her sister's credibility:

_____

_____

_____

_____

Use of compelling arguments:

_____

_____

_____

_____

_____

_____

_____

_____

Emotional response:

_____

_____

_____

_____

_____

_____

_____

Completion of sentences

1. Stanley's hands (p. 43, l. 3/p. 36, l. 15) have got a symbolic meaning because …

_____

_____

2. Blanche's remark "I was fishing for a compliment, Stanley" (p. 37, l. 9) is indicative of …

_____

_____

3. Stanley's refusal to compliment women on their looks is …

_____

_____

4. Stanley despises "glamour stuff" because …

_____

_____

5. When Stanley says that a woman has to "lay the cards on the table" (p. 38, l. 12), he makes it clear that …

_____

_____

6. By saying "My sister has married a man!" (p. 38, l. 19), Blanche intends to express that …

_____

_____

7. By spraying Stanley with her atomizer and calling him "a little boy" (p. 40, l. 19), Blanche makes it clear that …

_____

_____

8. Blanche's comments on her ancestors (p. 42) reveal …

_____

_____

9. By referring to the Napoleonic code and to his "lawyer acquaintance" (p. 43, l. 6), Stanley lays bare …

_____

_____

10. By treating her conversation with Stanley as a joke and flirting with him, Blanche …

_____

_____

die Lerngruppe in zwei Hälften geteilt, welche die zwischen Stella und Stanley bzw. zwischen Blanche und Stanley stattfindenden Unterhaltungen arbeitsteilig untersuchen. Um auch in großen Kursverbänden ein angemessen hohes Maß an Konzentration zu gewährleisten, sollten sich die Schülerinnen und Schüler innerhalb ihrer jeweiligen Gruppe der auf einem Arbeitsblatt zu bearbeitenden Aufgabe im Rahmen einer Partnerarbeit widmen. Somit ergehen folgende Arbeitsaufträge an die Lerngruppe:

Group 1, read p. 29– p. 35 (l. 11) and make notes on the worksheet (*Copy 3*). Work with your partner.
Group 2, read p. 35 (l. 12) – p. 44 and complete the following sentences (*Copy 4*). Work with your partner.

Arbeitsergebnisse von Gruppe 1 könnten wie folgt aussehen:

Lösungsvorschlag zu *Copy 3*:

The suspicions Blanche arouses in him: He suspects her of having sold the family mansion Belle Reve. More specifically, he supposes that Blanche has embezzled the proceeds she obtained when selling the estate.

Reasons for his suspicions: Although Blanche has allegedly lost the family mansion Belle Reve, she is in possession of elegant clothes, furs and jewellery. Moreover, it is not clear whether there are any documents that provide evidence of the loss of Belle Reve.

The way he shows his suspicions: By asking short and ominous questions such as "Yeah?", two times "So?" and "How?", Stanley indicates that he is calling Blanche's truthfulness into question. It seems that the vagueness of Stella's explanations come close to overtaxing his patience. To make clear that he is determined to discover Blanche's alleged "swindle", he threatens twice to consult experts about the value of her jewellery (p. 33, p. 34). In addition, raiding Blanche's trunk is a clear indication that he intends to leave no stone unturned in order to find out the truth about Blanche and the loss of Belle Reve. By referring to the Napoleonic code, he wants to convey the impression that he cannot be taken in because of his awareness of his rights.

The way Stella tries to dispel Stanley's doubts about her sister's credibility: On the one hand, she tries to sensitize Stanley to Blanche's frail condition und aims at reasoning him into a sensible course of action, but on the other hand, she scolds him and calls him names.

Use of compelling arguments: By pointing out that Blanche's "fox pieces" are "inexpensive summer furs" and that her jewellery is made from glass, she tries to convince Stanley of the worthlessness of her sister's accessories. Moreover, she sets out to make him realize that he has got sufficient time to ask her sister questions.

Emotional response: By calling him an "idiot" (p. 33) and labelling him as "ridiculous" (p. 32) as well as "stupid and horrid" (p. 34), Stella wants to lay emphasis on the absurdity of Stanley's suspicions and accusations.

Die von Gruppe 2 vorgenommene Vervollständigung der Satzanfänge könnte zu folgenden Ergebnissen geführt haben:

Lösungsvorschlag zu *Copy 4:*

1. ... they reflect his coarseness, tactlessness and lack of sensitivity in social intercourse with women.
2. ... her playfulness und flippancy. She seems to be teasing Stanley about his coarseness and clumsiness.
3. ... emblematic of his general attitude towards women. He expects them to submit to his superior strength and is not willing to make any concessions to them.
4. ... of its ambiguity, artificiality and pretentiousness. As someone who not only belongs to the working-class, but also has a working-class identity, he appreciates people that are practical, straightforward and down-to-earth.
5. ... truthfulness and authenticity are very important values for him. By uttering these words very slowly, he might indicate that he suspects Blanche of being dishonest.
6. ... Stanley is the incarnation of masculinity and virility. On the other hand, she might also be insinuating that Stanley's archetypical manliness makes him oblivious to subtle nuances of meaning.
7. ... she does not or does not want to take him seriously.
8. ... that she bears a grudge against them. Contrary to her general aura of prissiness and refinement, she does not recoil from using harsh words to describe her ancestors' failure and neglect.
9. ... his helplessness. Both his simplistic definition of the Napoleonic code und his need for a "lawyer acquaintance" reveal his lack of expertise. By issuing threats against Blanche, he lays himself open to ridicule.
10. ... strengthens Stanley's belief that she is a frivolous and untrustworthy person. Stanley's remark "If I didn't know that you was my wife's sister I'd get ideas about you!" (p. 39, ll. 22/23) undoubtedly bears evidence of his suspicion and distrust.

In Anbetracht der Tatsache, dass sich Blanche in Gegenwart ihrer Schwester Stella damit brüstet, Stanley und seine Verdächtigungen nicht ernst genommen zu haben und somit andeutet, dass sie sich im Gespräch mit ihm unzweifelhaft überlegen gefühlt hat, sollten die Schülerinnen und Schüler ihrerseits eine Bewertung des Gespräches zwischen Blanche und Stanley vornehmen. Da auch Stella im weiteren Verlauf des Dramas eine Schlüsselfunktion zukommt, die es zu definieren bzw. zu bestimmen gilt, sollten die Schülerinnen und Schüler auch ihr Gespräch mit Stanley einer Bewertung unterziehen.

Um zu einem möglichst lebhaften Gedankenaustausch anzuregen, wird folgende Fragestellung im Plenum diskutiert:

Who dominates the conversation that is held
a) by Stanley and Blanche?
b) by Stanley and Stella?

Die zu erwartenden Schülerbeiträge könnten in folgendem Tafelbild münden:

Stanley	**Blanche**
dominates the conversation because	dominates the conversation hecause
• Blanche does not manage to make him exchange light-hearted banter with him • by not complimenting Blanche on her looks, he proves to be stubborn and consistent	• she holds Stanley's machismo and suspicion up to ridicule • her openness about the loss of Belle Reve not only disarms Stanley, but also shames him into giving rather humble explanations for his behaviour
Stanley	**Stella**
dominates the conversation because	dominates the conversation because
• he makes Stella lose her temper • he forces Stella to fight in her sister's corner • Stella does not manage to persuade him into abstaining from interrogating her sister	• a large number of her statements prove to be factual and convincing

Ausgehend von der Annahme, dass die Mehrzahl der Schülerinnen und Schüler den Eindruck gewonnen haben, Blanche sei Stanley aufgrund ihrer entwaffnenden Offenheit und ihrer subtilen Ironie überlegen, erscheint es von sehr großer Wichtigkeit zu sein, die Aufmerksamkeit der Lerngruppe zum Abschluss der Stunde auf eine Aussage zu lenken, die Blanche am Ende von Szene 2 gegenüber ihrer Schwester Stella macht:

> "He's just not the sort that goes for jasmine perfume! But maybe he's what we need to mix with our blood now that we've lost Belle Reve and have to go on without Belle Reve to protect us …" (p. 44, ll. 11–14)

Da die oben zitierte Äußerung Blanches nicht nur in teilweisem Widerspruch zu dem augenscheinlichen Gefühl der Überlegenheit, welches sie gegenüber Stanley hegt, zu stehen scheint, sondern darüber hinaus auch in einem engen Zusammenhang mit dem in der zweiten Hälfte des 19. Jahrhunderts gewachsenen Selbstverständnis des amerikanischen Südens steht, sollten die Schülerinnen und Schüler in die Lage versetzt werden, neben der persönlichen auch die historische Dimension des Zitats zu erkennen. Der an die Lerngruppe ergehende Arbeitsauftrag sollte somit sicherstellen, dass sowohl auf die durch das zu Beginn der Stunde gehaltene Referat vermittelten Kenntnisse als auch auf die von den Schülerinnen und Schülern im Verlaufe der Stunde erarbeiteten Ergebnisse zurückgegriffen werden kann.

Es ergehen somit folgende Arbeitsaufträge an die Lerngruppe, die in Partnerarbeit zu erledigen sind:

1. Find out what Blanche's statement reveals about her personality.

2. Link Blanche's statement to American history.

Die von den Schülerinnen und Schülern im Plenum präsentierten Ergebnisse sollten folgende zentralen Erkenntnisse enthalten:

Zu 1:
Blanche's personality:
- she seems to be rather volatile because her statement is in sharp contrast to the utter contempt she shows for Stanley in scene 1 ("Polack")
- she has got a defeatist attitude because she makes it clear that she and her sister are in no position to regain their former wealth and status
- she is philosophical about her own and Stella's situation

Zu 2:
Link to American history:
- Since the South's crushing defeat in the American Civil War (1865) was not only followed by the establishment of governments dominated by Northerners, but also entailed adopting Northern ideas and values, the South gradually lost a large part of its identity and sovereignty.
  Having lost her property and being at the mercy of a man who is the embodiment of Northern pragmatism and vigour, Blanche seems to be a perfect example of the disillusioned and impoverished Southerner.

Eingedenk der Tatsache, dass sich die ironische Distanz und Toleranz, mit welcher Blanche der Rohheit und Taktlosigkeit Stanleys in Szene 2 begegnet, angesichts seines brutalen und handgreiflichen Vorgehens gegen Stella in den Szenen 3 und 4 in pures Entsetzen und flammenden Klassenhass wandelt, lesen die Schülerinnen und Schüler Szene 3 im Rahmen einer Hausaufgabe unter folgenden Aufgabenstellungen:

1. Summarize scenes 3 and 4.

2. What is/are the most crucial incident(s)/development(s) in scenes 3 and 4? Give reasons for your choice.

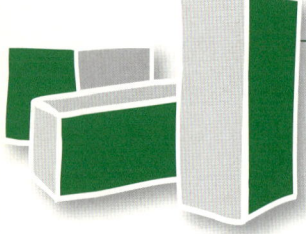

Domestic violence and hope for a better future

2.1 The poker night and its implications

Die als Einleitung in die Besprechung der Szenen 3 und 4 dienenden und im Rahmen der Hausaufgabe angefertigten Zusammenfassungen sollten folgende inhaltliche Aspekte berücksichtigen:

> Scene 3:
>
> - Blanche and Stella have enjoyed a night out at the theatre and return to Elysian Fields
> - the poker game is still going on
> - Stanley has had too much to drink and is resentful of Mitch's interest in Blanche
> - to give vent to his pent up anger Stanley throws Stella's radio out of the window
> - Stella starts remonstrating angrily with Stanley and is beaten up by him
> - although Stella temporarily seeks refuge in Eunice's apartment, she returns to her husband in the same night
> - outraged at her sister's inconsistency, Blanche has to be calmed down by Mitch
>
> Scene 4:
>
> - Blanche tries to persuade Stella into leaving Stanley, but Stella refuses
> - Stanley overhears Blanche's attempts to denigrate him by portraying him as a contemptible brute

Hinsichtlich der Bestimmung der zentralsten Ereignisse bzw. Entwicklungen im Verlaufe der Szenen 3 und 4 könnten die Schülerinnen und Schüler zu folgenden Ergebnissen gekommen sein:

> The most crucial incidents/developments in scenes 3 and 4:
>
> - Stanley's outburst of violence because it makes us aware of his dangerousness and brutality
> - Stella's return to her husband because it gives us a deep insight into the strength of her passion for Stanley
> - Blanche's showing interest in the shy Mitch because it shows that – contrary to her genteel manner – she is in fact rather frivolous and flirtatious
> - Stanley's eavesdropping on the conversation held by Stella and Blanche because this incident not only clarifies the relations between the main characters even further, but also foreshadows imminent conflicts and clashes

Nachdem die Schülerinnen und Schüler die Handlungsverläufe der Szenen 3 und 4 zusammengefasst und zentrale Ereignisse bewertet haben, sollte nunmehr das Augenmerk der Lerngruppe auf die sich in den Szenen manifestierenden sozialen und verbalen Interaktionen sowie die sich immer klarer herausstellenden charakterlichen Dispositionen der Protagonisten gelenkt werden. Dies ist insbesondere deshalb von zentraler Bedeutung, weil Blanches Unfähigkeit, die in Stanleys und Stellas Ehe bzw. in deren Milieu geltenden Regeln zu verstehen und die hiermit in engem Zusammenhang stehende nahende Katastrophe sich schon in den Szenen 3 und 4 abzuzeichnen beginnt. Blanches fehlender Scharfblick zeigt sich unter anderem in ihrer auf Mitch bezogenen Aussage „That one seems – superior to the others" (p. 50, l. 6) und der Tatsache, dass sie die augenscheinliche Dominanz, die Stanley gegenüber Mitch und den anderen Pokerfreunden ausübt, nicht zu realisieren scheint. Dies sollte Anlass dazu geben, den Hintergrund bzw. die Ursachen der von ihr getroffenen Aussage näher zu beleuchten. Zu diesem Zweck untersuchen die Schülerinnen und Schüler zunächst sowohl die Atmosphäre, welche das Pokerspiel der in Stanleys Küche versammelten Männer prägt, als auch die im Rahmen des Kartenspiels geführte Konversation. Um einen möglichst differenzierten Blick auf die sich während des Pokerspiels abzeichnenden Regeln, Hierarchien und Verhaltensmuster zu gewähren, werden die Schülerinnen und Schüler zunächst angewiesen, das in der Bühnenanweisung auf Seite 45 erwähnte und im Vorfeld ausgehändigte Bild van Goghs *The Night Cafe in the Place Lamartine in Arles* (*Copy 5*) zu betrachten und zu den in Stanleys Küche versammelten Pokerspielern in Bezug zu setzen. Somit ergeht folgender Arbeitsauftrag an die Lerngruppe:

> Read the stage directions on page 45 and look at the picture by van Gogh that the stage directions allude to. What do Williams' description of the poker players and van Gogh's picture have in common? What is different?

Die von den Schülerinnen und Schülern hervorgebrachten Eindrücke bzw. Ergebnisse könnten in folgendem Tafelbild münden:

Van Gogh's picture – Williams' description

Similarities
- glaring light
- bottles and glasses on the table(s)
- the spectator's/ reader's attention is drawn to the game that can be/is about to be played in the kitchen/billiard parlour

Differences
- distinct from the soporific atmosphere that dominates van Gogh's picture, Williams' description radiates nervous energy
- while the poker players are gathered at one table, the people in van Gogh's picture are sitting at different tables and thus give the impression of being dispersed
- whereas the poker players' attention is focused on their game, the people in van Gogh's picture seem to be lethargic, impassive and indifferent
- while the poker players seem to form a homogeneous group (similar clothes, similar physiognomy, etc.), van Gogh's picture shows a man who is set apart from the other people in the billiard parlour
(aside from the fact that he is the only person that is standing, his elegant white suit and his nonchalance distinguish him from the other people in the picture)

Vincent van Gogh (1853–1890),
The Night Café in the Place Lamartine in Arles, c. 1888

Angesichts der Tatsache, dass die Bühnenanweisung auf Seite 45 nicht nur den Eindruck von Homogenität sowie Uniformität vermittelt, sondern unterschwellig auch auf eine aggressive Spannung hindeutet, die sich möglicherweise im Verlaufe des Pokerspiels entlädt, sollte die Lektüre der Seiten 46–49 von folgenden Aufgabenstellungen begleitet werden:

1. Do the stage directions on page 45 contain hints that the poker game cannot develop in a peaceful and harmonious manner? Give reasons.

2. Read pages 46–49 and find adjectives that help to characterize the poker players.

Während die im Rahmen der Bearbeitung von Aufgabe 1 vorgebrachten Schüleräußerungen (wie z. B. "Yes, because adjectives such as *coarse, powerful* and *direct* hint at a certain aggressiveness on the poker players' part. Their aggressiveness might lead them to quarrel.") im Plenum gesammelt werden können, sollten die bezüglich der Pokerspieler getroffenen Aussagen an der Tafel aufgelistet werden, um sie im Nachhinein vor dem Hintergrund der von Blanche auf S. 50 geäußerten Einschätzung "That one seems – superior to the other" beleuchten zu können.

Die von den Schülerinnen und Schülern gewählten und auf die Pokerspieler bezogenen Adjektive könnten in folgender Übersicht aufgelistet werden:

Stanley	Pablo	Steve	Mitch
• aggressive • irritable • overbearing • hot-headed • domineering (he bosses his friends about) • rude • impolite (his behaviour is offensive)	• his focus of attention/ interest is the poker game and his physical well-being → he is <u>oblivious</u> to things that are not closely connected to the poker game	• cheerful • hilarious (he cracks jokes) • Stanley's impatience and aggressiveness do not disturb him → imperturbable • serene • well-balanced	• careful • wary • concerned about his mother • he does not share the other men's enthusiasm for the poker game → sober, rational • he is awkward and polite in the presence of Stella and Blanche

Da die Gegenüberstellung der herausgearbeiteten Eigenschaften der Pokerspieler Stanley, Pablo, Steve und Mitch mit Blanches Aussage "That one seems – superior to the others" zu unterschiedlichen Einschätzungen und Kommentaren führen könnte, ist es wichtig, Blanches Aussage nicht nur daraufhin zu überprüfen, ob sie zutrifft, sondern darüber hinaus auch zu ergründen, warum sie diesen Eindruck gewinnt. Aus diesem Grund sollte die Lerngruppe folgende Fragestellungen im Plenum diskutieren:

1. Do you think Blanche's impression that Mitch is superior to the other poker players is correct/justified? Give reasons.

2. What might be the reasons for Blanche's judgement?

Folgende Schülerbeiträge sind zu erwarten:

Zu 1:
• As a bachelor who lives with his mother, Mitch is not superior to the others; he is simply different to them. (NO!)

- Since Mitch is neither quick-witted nor quick at repartee, he is not able to put up much resistance to Stanley's insults and accusations. (NO!)
- Compared to his hot-blooded and vulgar friends, Mitch seems to be rather rational and aloof. These qualities make him appear to be less puerile and narrow-minded than Stanley and the other poker players. For this reason, he might be regarded as superior to them. (YES!)

Zu 2:
Blanche apparently appreciates Mitch's politeness and discretion. Since these qualities are often associated with good breeding, Blanche considers Mitch to be superior to the other poker players.

Die von den Schülern geleisteten Beiträge sollen in der Folge herangezogen werden, um die sich zwischen Mitch und Blanche anbahnende Liaison näher zu untersuchen. Dies ist insbesondere deshalb von zentraler Bedeutung, weil das für den Verlauf der Dramenhandlung so entscheidende Nichtzustandekommen einer langfristigen Beziehung zwischen Mitch und Blanche eng mit deren Sichtweisen sowie Charaktereigenschaften verbunden ist. Um den Schülerinnen und Schülern einen möglichst eigenständigen Umgang mit den Besonderheiten der Charaktere Mitch und Blanche zu ermöglichen, bearbeiten sie im Rahmen einer Partnerarbeit folgende Aufgabenstellung:

Read the conversation that Mitch has with Blanche (p. 53, l. 16 – p. 63). Imagine you are the owner of a marriage agency which Blanche and Mitch have visited independently of each other. After their respective visits, you and your colleague discuss the question of whether they might turn out to be a well-matched couple. Make up a dialogue.

Der von den Schülerinnen und Schülern in der Folge verfasste Dialog könnte folgende Abwägungen enthalten:

<u>Yes</u>, they might turn out to be a well-matched couple <u>because</u>
- Mitch can give support to the unstable, indecisive and unbalanced Blanche
- Blanche's vivaciousness might cheer Mitch up and give him a new lease of life
- Mitch might make Blanche understand the outlook, mentality and values of the people that live in Stella and Stanley's quarter, thus she might be inclined to he more tolerant of her sister's life-style and her marriage to Stanley

<u>No</u>, they will not turn out to be a well-matched couple <u>because</u>
- Mitch cannot overcome the class differences between him and Blanche
- in the long run, it will be too difficult for Mitch to come to terms with the inconsistencies in Blanche's behaviour (on the one hand, she is the genteel Southern Lady who expects men to stand up when she enters a room and who cannot bear a rude remark or a vulgar action, but on the other hand, she has the air of a cheap seductress)
- Blanche's lies about her age, her equally false claim that she has come to Elysian Fields to help her sister and her obsession with her physical

appearance are incompatible with Mitch's sincerity and down-to-earth approach to daily life
● Blanche does not fit in with Mitch's social surroundings

In den Dialogen ist möglicherweise das fehlende Verständnis Blanches für die in Elysian Fields geltenden Regeln und Werte angeklungen. Da unterschiedliche Wertvorstellungen in der Folge zu einer unüberwindbaren Kluft zwischen den Schwestern führen, sollten die Schülerinnen und Schüler erkennen, dass Blanches Entsetzen über die körperliche Gewalt, welcher ihrer Schwester durch Stanley widerfährt und ihre in Szene 4 unternommenen Versuche, Stella dazu zu bewegen, Stanley zu verlassen, Anzeichen einer zwischen den Schwestern eingetretenen Entfremdung sind. Zu diesem Zweck lesen sie im Rahmen einer Hausaufgabe die Seiten 58 – 76 unter folgenden Aufgabenstellungen:

Comment on the following statement:
Due to their common background and the social values they were brought up with, one might consider Stella and Blanche to be very much alike, but in fact they are vastly different. The sisters' reactions to Stanley's outburst of violence shows that there is no common ground between them.

Der von den Schülerinnen und Schülern verfasste Kommentar könnte folgende Gestalt annehmen:

Although the statement at hand is one that at first glance looks like a sweeping generalization, it actually proves to be tenable. As a matter of fact, it is not merely the bitter dispute over Stella's decision to rush back into Stanley's arms despite having been beaten up by him that illustrates the gaping abyss between the two sisters, but also their incapability of finding a common language. While Blanche, owing to her strong affinity for literature, tends to make use of a language abounding in metaphors and connotative expressions ("… he's common … ordinary … just plain … bestial … sub-human … a survivor of the stone age! Bearing the raw meat home from the kill in the jungle!", p. 74, l. 3 – l. 10), Stella, in contrast, confines herself to terse and laconic phrases that are indicative of her matter-of-fact approach to personal affairs. Her life with Stanley seems to have endowed her with the equilibrium and balanced state of mind that Blanche is entirely lacking in. Stella's reading comics, on the other hand, is both a clear indication that she does not harbour any intellectual ambition at all and a silent reminder that she has accepted a world in which cheap entertainment prevails over sophistication.
Blanche, who is outraged by her sister's calm acceptance of her husband's standards und values cannot or does not want to understand the reasons for Stella's compliance. Thus, her dismissal of Stella's remark "But there are things that happen between a man and a woman in the dark – that sort of make everything else seem unimportant" (p. 72. l. 29 – p. 73, l. 2) as "brutal desire" (p. 73, l. 3) is either symptomatic of her complete obliviousness to true passion or utter hatred for her animalistic brother-in-law Stanley. In this connection, it should be noted that the very fact that even Stella labels Stanley as an animal "Drunk-drunk-animal thing, you!" (p. 58, l. 16) when he throws her radio out of the window indicates the unbridgeable contrasts between the two sisters. While for Stella, the noun "animal" connotes wild und untamed manliness, Blanche

merely associates it with deliberate cruelty and horrifying bestiality. In actual fact, although both women condemn violence, Stella displays this characteristic less strongly than Blanche. The reason for this might be the vastly different experiences she has had with regard to love, passion und desire.

2.2 The function of men in Blanche's life (scene 5)

Wie keine andere Szene in Williams Drama offenbart Szene 5 die zentrale sowie ambivalente Rolle, welche Männer in Blanches Leben spielen. Obschon sie für Blanche einerseits Schutz, Geborgenheit sowie soziale Sicherheit verkörpern, sind sie auf der anderen Seite unerbittliche Gradmesser für körperliche Attraktivität sowie harte Verhandlungspartner, deren Zuwendung nur durch sexuelle Dienste erkauft werden kann. Das sich hierin spiegelnde Dilemma Blanches, soziale Sicherheit erlangen zu wollen, ohne jedoch die persönliche Ehre bzw. den guten Ruf aufs Spiel zu setzen, wird durch ihren zwanghaften Drang, sich durch ständige Flirts mit einer Vielzahl von Männern ihrer körperlichen Anziehungskraft zu vergewissern, sichtbar. Um die Schülerinnen und Schüler für diese Tragik in Blanches Leben zu sensibilisieren, werden sie zunächst aufgefordert, Szene 5 zu lesen und die Rolle bzw. Funktion aller in der Szene auftretenden bzw. erwähnten Männer zu definieren. Im Falle von Stanley und Shep Huntleigh ist es von großer Wichtigkeit, dass die Lerngruppe sich nochmals Stanleys unmittelbare Reaktion auf Blanches Verunglimpfungen „Hiyuh, Blanche. (He grins at her)" (p. 76, l. 5) und Blanches Erzählungen von Shep Huntleigh (p. 68, l. 23– p. 70) vergegenwärtigen. Somit ergeht folgender Arbeitsauftrag an die Schülerinnen und Schüler:

> Read scene 5 und pay attention to all the men that appear on stage as well as the men that are merely mentioned. What function do they have for Blanche? Draw up a list. When referring to Stanley and Shep Huntleigh, take a closer look at p. 76, l. 5 und p. 68, l. 22– p. 70.

Die von den Schülerinnen und Schülern zu erstellende Auflistung sollte sich auf folgende Aspekte konzentrieren:

Stanley:
Stanley embodies everything that Blanche despises: He is rude, cruel, uneducated and lacks sensitivity. Since he is set to reveal compromising details about her past, he also threatens to blemish her reputation.

Steve:
His coarseness and simple-mindedness seem to provoke a feeling of superiority in Blanche. Like a scientist investigating a new animal species, she sets out to note down the funny expressions he uses.

Shep Huntleigh:
According to Blanche, Shep Huntleigh is an incredibly rich man who used to date her when she was young. Although one might raise doubts about the truthfulness of the accounts she gives about a meeting she has had with him quite recently, it is beyond doubt that Shep Huntleigh plays an important role in her life. As a representative of the upper class, he not only reminds her of her own social background, but also represents the

ideal husband to strive for. A man like him would be able to offer Blanche sanctuary and thus would spare her the ordeal she has to undergo at her sister's place.

A certain Mr Shaw/various men at a hotel called Flamingo:
At first glance, these are men who had promiscuous relationships with Blanche and thus are able to blemish her reputation. However, in taking a closer look at the things that Blanche utters on p. 83, it becomes apparent that the affairs with these men not only stand for her social decline, but also symbolize her dilemma/personal tragedy. Living in the constant fear of losing her good looks, she is on a frantic search for men who can give her reassurance that she is still attractive. Unfortunately, though, since that kind of behaviour is regarded as promiscuous and hence carries a social stigma, she thereby forfeits a promising future with a husband who could offer her the much longed-for home where she could settle down und live free of financial concerns.

Young man:
Blanche's encounter with the young man indicates that her behaviour in the presence of men is comparable to a reflex action. As soon as she is confronted with the opposite sex, she cannot help but being flirtatious and frivolous. Feeling very strongly attracted to the young man might also have something to do with the resemblance he bears to her late husband, as the young man might remind her of the deep love she used to feel towards her husband.

Mitch:
Blanche's hopes of marrying Mitch seem to spring from her desperation in the face of Stanley's veiled threats about divulging details of her promiscuous behaviour in Laurel. Since the startling revelations concerning her past might induce Stanley to throw her out of his flat, she seeks refuge in the arms of someone who obviously feels attracted to her and who might be able to save her from being at Stanley's mercy. Nevertheless, her flirting with a young man prior to her date with Mitch shows that her wish to marry him has nothing to do with love.

Angesichts des Wechselbads von Gefühlen, welchem Blanche im Verlaufe von Szene 5 ausgesetzt ist, und der sich hierin widerspiegelnden Volatilität, Verzweiflung und Zerrissenheit, sollte im weiteren Unterrichtsverlauf Blanches Gemütszustand einer näheren Analyse unterzogen werden. Da Blanches abrupte Stimmungswechsel besonders in ihrem Gespräch mit Stella manifest werden, lesen die Schülerinnen und Schüler die Konversation der beiden Schwestern unter folgender Aufgabenstellung:

> Read the conversation between Blanche und Stella on pages 82–87 and decide which of the following adjectives best serves to reflect Blanche's state of mind. Give reasons for your choice.

Eine Liste mit Adjektiven, aus der die Schülerinnen und Schüler auswählen können, ist bei Bedarf vorzugeben. Sie könnte u. a. folgende Adjektive enthalten:

> depressed, dejected, resigned, nervous, indifferent, optimistic, well-balanced, honest

Die im Plenum vorgestellten Schülerbeiträge sollten auf einer den Schülerinnen und Schülern zur Verfügung gestellten Folie oder an der Tafel festgehalten werden. Folgende Lösungsvorschläge sind zu erwarten:

> Blanche is <u>desperate</u> and <u>depressed</u> about the prospect of losing her good looks, for this might ultimately deprive her of the opportunity to be adored by a respectable man.
>
> Since she does not try to hide the reasons for her being so sensitive about her age, she can be regarded as <u>honest</u>.
>
> She is <u>frightened</u> of being found out by Stanley and dreads the humiliation of being turned out by him.
>
> Losing her grip on the glass of Coca-Cola that is handed to her by Stella and spilling its contents over her dress is indicative of her utter <u>nervousness</u> und emotional turmoil.
>
> Uttering the interjection "ah, me" at the close of the conversation with Stella might demonstrate that she is <u>resigned</u> and <u>desperate</u>.

Da das in der vorangegangenen Unterrichtssequenz zur Sprache gekommene Verschütten eines mit Cola gefüllten Glases nicht nur Ausdruck von Blanches Nervosität und innerer Unruhe ist, sondern darüber hinaus auch als eine vielsagende Metapher für ihre Lebenssituation gesehen werden muss, sollten die Schülerinnen und Schüler im Rahmen eines Unterrichtsgesprächs auf diesen Umstand aufmerksam gemacht werden. Folgende Aufgabenstellung sollte somit in diesem Zusammenhang bearbeitet werden:

> Take a close look at the passage which deals with Blanche's spilling Coca-Cola over her dress. Apart from Blanche's nervousness and inner turmoil, what else strikes you about the significance of the incident and Blanche's reactions (p. 85)?

Von Seiten der Schülerinnen und Schüler zu erwartende Beiträge wie beispielsweise „the incident symbolizes Blanche's past, Blanche gives a piercing cry" oder „Blanche's dismay is indicative of her fear of blemishes on her reputation" könnte in folgendem Tafelbild münden:

Incident/reactions:	Blanche spills coke on her white dress	Blanche gives a piercing cry	Blanche manages to remove the stain on her dress
Metaphorical meaning:	Blanche's promiscuous behaviour (particularly in Laurel) has gained her a bad reputation. Her sojourn in Laurel can be seen as a spot on her reputation. Blemishes on her skin hint at her fading beauty → Her body is starting to show signs of age.	The cry reveals her deep-seated trauma about having stained her honour and reputation.	The metaphorical meaning is closely connected to her forthcoming rendezvous with Mitch. Up to now, she has been able to conceal her promiscuous behaviour and her true age from him.

Die von Blanche als Ausdruck von Verzweiflung und Resignation hervorgebrachte Interjektion „ah, me" (S. 87, Z. 1), welcher voraussichtlich ohne die durch das Kichern der schwarzen Frau verursachte Ablenkung weitere Worte gefolgt wären, soll schließlich Anlass dazu geben, den Schülerinnen und Schülern die Möglichkeit zu geben, einen Monolog zu schreiben, der Blanches Lebenssituation und Gemütszustand reflektiert. Dieses Vorgehen fördert nicht nur den kreativen Umgang mit der Fremdsprache, sondern ermöglicht darüber hinaus eine intensive Auseinandersetzung mit Blanches Sicht auf ihre Vergangenheit, Gegenwart und Zukunft. Somit ergeht folgender Arbeitsauftrag an die Lerngruppe:

> After Blanche has uttered the interjection "ah, me" she starts soliloquizing. Her soliloquy comprises thoughts about her past, present and future. Write a soliloquy on her behalf. (It has to become apparent that she is aware of being placed in a dilemma und afraid of not being able to prevent tragic events.)

Der von den Schülerinnen und Schülern verfasste Monolog könnte folgende Form annehmen:

> ... ah, me ... the sense of an impending revelation and my anxiety about my rendezvous with Mitch seem to be too much for me. But, on the other hand, if some great change is pending in my life, I have to regard it as a challenge to which I have to respond boldly. If I think about it most profoundly it has often occurred to me that my miserable situation has a lot to do with my being faced with a constant dilemma. The flamboyant and flirtatious Southern Belle has to coexist in me with a timid, conscientious person full of moral scruples and conventional fears. I feel the strong urge to do something, to act, which often afflicts people in unresolvable dilemmas. If one could only act, flee, settle down, live free of financial concerns, one could ease the anxiety, an anxiety which is really nothing more than a fear of the future in the form of a fear of the darkness of one's present desires: "dread", such as philosophers speak of, is not so much really an experience of void as the appalling sense that one is in the grip of some very strong as yet undeclared motive.

Um eine angemessene Grundlage für die Analyse des in Szene 6 beschriebenen Rendezvous von Blanche und Mitch zu haben, resümieren die Schülerinnen und Schüler die genannte Szene im Rahmen eine Hausaufgabe:

> Summarize scene 6.

2.3 The rendezvous (scene 6)

Die von den Schülerinnen und Schülern im Rahmen der Hausaufgabe angefertigten Zusammenfassungen (siehe 2.2) könnte wie folgt aussehen:

> On their return from a night out, Blanche and Mitch awkwardly own up to the fact that the evening they have spent together has been a letdown. In a rather desperate attempt to lighten Mitch's mood, Blanche reassures him that she does not resent the advances he has made to her. To prove that she does not bear any resentment towards him, she invites Mitch

in for a nightcap. The ensuing conversation in Stella's kitchen, which at first turns out to be rather awkward und embarrassing, gradually develops into a serious exchange of ideas, experiences and fears. At the end of their intimate talk, Mitch suggests marriage.

Auf Basis der von den Schülerinnen und Schülern angefertigten Zusammenfassungen soll im Folgenden das Verhalten bzw. das Zusammenspiel der Figuren Mitch und Blanche vor dem Hintergrund atmosphärischer Schwingungen, welche die Unterredung der beiden begleiten, beleuchtet werden. Zu diesem Zweck wird den Schülerinnen und Schülern ein Arbeitsblatt (*Copy 6*) an die Hand gegeben, auf welchem Satzfragmente abgedruckt sind, deren korrekte Vervollständigung zu präzisen Aussagen über Blanche, Mitch und die Atmosphäre ihres Zusammenseins führen. Da die Schülerinnen bei der Vervollständigung der Satzfragmente dazu angehalten sind, ihre jeweiligen Ergänzungen am Ausgangstext zu belegen, werden nicht nur ihre Fertigkeiten im Hinblick auf das Finden präziser Formulierungen geschult, sondern es wird ihnen darüber hinaus auch nochmals die zentrale Wichtigkeit des *Close Reading* vor Augen geführt.

Für die Bearbeitung von *Copy 6* wären folgende Lösungen denkbar:

1. … downbeat and depressing. Mitch seems to be more subdued than usual and although Blanche tries to cheer Mitch up, the reader detects that it takes her concerted efforts to lift the mood.
2. … as a kind of code that helps her to express her thoughts and feelings without offending Mitch or letting him in on her secrets. Thus, in taking advantage of Mitch's ignorance, she subconsciously stresses the difference between their cultural, social und educational backgrounds.
3. … indicative of his obsession with his physique. Sporting his muscular body and taking pride in his strength, he apparently aims at impressing Blanche. His admission that he is ashamed of his strong perspiration, however, reveals him to be very self-conscious und insecure.
4. … indicative of her inability to come to terms with her true age. Thus, labelling herself as a girl is a desperate attempt to escape from reality.
5. … be indicative of her great capacity for giving people courage und confidence. Nevertheless, although she compliments Mitch on his physique, it is not quite clear whether Mitch's muscular body und his strength are a source of admiration or ridicule to her. "Samson! Go on, lift me." (p. 97, l. 16)
6. … ironic. By rolling her eyes self-mockingly and unseen by Mitch when she speaks these words, she makes it clear that she is well-aware of the fact that, due to her promiscuous behaviour, she has more or less barred herself from polite society. Blanche's frivolity and insincerity in Mitch's presence are also further proof of her not taking him seriously.
7. … met with blank incomprehension. Mitch is neither able to conceive why Stanley might hate Blanche nor does he understand her subtly hinted at conjecture that Stanley's dislike of her might, to a certain degree, be rooted in a perverse sexual attraction. Subtleties of that kind are beyond Mitch's grasp.
8. … at a possible reason for her volatility, restlessness and inconsistencies. The traumatic experience of her husband's death and her role in

The atmosphere between Blanche and Mitch

Complete the sentences and support your solutions with evidence from the text.

1. The opening mood of scene 6 is ...

_____

_____

_____

_____

2. Blanche's use of the French language and her quoting of literary works serves ...

_____

_____

_____

_____

3. The information und details that Mitch gives about himself and his life are ...

_____

_____

_____

_____

4. Blanche's habit of referring to herself as a girl is ...

_____

_____

_____

_____

5. Blanche's reactions to Mitch's confessions might ...

_____

_____

_____

_____

6. Blanche's statement that she has old-fashioned ideals is …

_____

_____

_____

_____

7. Blanche's assumption that Stanley hates her is …

_____

_____

_____

_____

8. Blanche's story about her former husband hints …

_____

_____

_____

_____

9. By suggesting that he would like to marry Blanche, Mitch gives …

_____

_____

_____

_____

the affair have been so shocking and upsetting to her that they still seem to affect her.

9. ... evidence of his openness and naivety. Although Blanche's pretentiousness and frivolity lead him to believe she is an eligible woman to marry, Mitch seems to be completely oblivious to her less attractive traits.

Da die Frivolität und mangelnde Ernsthaftigkeit, welche Blanche in Szene 6 teilweise gegenüber Mitch an den Tag legt, in auffälligem Kontrast stehen zu der Rührung und Verzückung, mit welcher sie Mitchs indirekten Heiratsantrag am Ende der Szene entgegennimmt, sollten die Schülerinnen und Schüler in die Lage versetzt werden, etwaige Ursachen für ihr Verhalten zu suchen. Um eine möglichst vielschichtige Diskussion in Gang zu bringen, diskutieren die Schülerinnen und Schüler zunächst folgende Fragestellung im Plenum:

> Does Blanche's reaction to Mitch's marriage proposal come as a surprise to you? Give reasons for your answer.

Etwaige Schüleräußerungen wie z. B. „Her reaction is surprising because throughout the scene she has given the impression of not being able to face the humdrum ordinary demands that a life with Mitch would entail" oder „Taking into account her volatility and inconsistencies, her reaction comes as a surprise", etc. sollen schließlich in der Analyse der konkreten Bedeutung, welche Blanches Ausruf „Sometimes – there's God – so quickly" (S. 104, Z. 17) hat, münden. Aufgrund der Tatsache, dass der Begriff *God* mannigfaltige bzw. weitreichende Assoziationen weckt, werden die Schülerinnen und Schüler zunächst aufgefordert im Sinne eines *brainstorming* Eindrücke, Ideen und Vorstellungen zu sammeln, die sie mit dem genannten Begriff verbinden:

> What associations does the word *God* have for you?

Die von den Schülerinnen und Schülern genannten Vorstellungen bzw. Assoziationen werden an der Tafel gesammelt:

```
                      guidance
         trust                      forgiveness
   faith              God                  sanctuary
       salvation                  clemency
              unconditional love
```

In einem nächsten Unterrichtsschritt sollen die Schülerinnen und Schüler schließlich ihre Assoziationen hinsichtlich des Begriffes *God* mit dem Leben Blanches in Verbindung bringen. Somit ergeht folgender Arbeitsauftrag an die Lerngruppe:

> Explain why the ideas and associations connected to the word *God* are important for Blanche's life.

Folgende Erklärungen wären denkbar:

- Blanche needs <u>forgiveness</u> because she has led a sinful life.
- Blanche has to find <u>sanctuary</u> because she needs protection against

> people like Stanley who intend to denigrate her by revealing compromising details about her past.
> - Blanche has a strong need for <u>unconditional love</u> because, in her experience, men have always tended to take advantage of her weaknesses.
> - Since her life lacks direction, she needs somebody who can guide her. In other words, she needs moral <u>guidance</u> to make her way in the world.

Die von den Schülerinnen und Schülern angeführten Erklärungen werden im Anschluss an der Tafel oder auf einer Folie gesammelt und dienen als Übersicht über Funktionen, die Mitch in Blanches Leben zu erfüllen vermag. Somit werden die Schülerinnen und Schüler darauffolgend mit folgender Fragestellung konfrontiert:

Is Mitch capable of offering Blanche forgiveness, sanctuary, unconditional love, direction und moral guidance?

Die im Plenum möglicherweise kontrovers diskutierte Fragestellung könnte in folgendem Tafelbild münden:

What Mitch can(not) offer to Blanche

Forgiveness

Yes
- since he is very kind and gentle, he might stretch a point and forgive Blanche her promiscuous behaviour

No
- since he has rather provincial attitudes and, what is more, adheres to rigid moral principles, he is not very likely to forgive Blanche for her loose morals

Sanctuary

Yes
- his height and physical strength might give Blanche the feeling of being protected

No
- his lack of self-confidence, education and wealth make it impossible for him to offer Blanche the kind of security she is yearning for

Unconditional love

Yes
- his intense devotion to Blanche and his intention to marry her can be regarded as a token of his unconditional love

No
- since Mitch is under Stanley's steady influence, his friend's bad opinion of Blanche might eventually make him lose his love for her

Moral guidance

Yes
- –

No
- both his awkwardness in the presence of Blanche and his search for reassurance about his outward appearance are indicative of his self-consciousness and his feelings of insecurity; far from being able to guide Blanche, he seems to be the one in need of guidance; moreover, Blanche does not take him seriously

Component 2: Domestic violence and hope for a better future

Die von den Schülerinnen und Schülern im Verlaufe der Diskussion aller Voraussicht nach gestellte Prognose, dass Mitch nicht in der Lage sein wird, Blanche als moralische Leitfigur oder als Beschützer zu dienen (siehe Tafelbild), soll schließlich zum Anlass genommen werden, die Frage zu erörtern, was genau Blanche zu der Äußerung „Sometimes – there's God – so quickly!" (S. 104, Z. 17) bewegt haben mag. Somit diskutieren die Schülerinnen und Schüler abschließend folgende Fragestellung im Plenum:

> ### What might have caused Blanche's strong emotional response to Mitch's marriage proposal?

Blanches Neigung, Zuflucht in imaginären Traumwelten zu suchen, sollte bei der Beantwortung der Frage eine entscheidende Rolle spielen, denn es ist im Grunde nicht die Aussicht auf eine Heirat mit Mitch, welche Blanche in Verzückung versetzt, sondern vielmehr die Symbolhaftigkeit des von Mitch unterbreiteten Antrags. Vorstellungen wie Ansehen, Respektabilität und finanzielle Sicherheit, welche Blanche möglicherweise mit der Institution Ehe verbindet, sind im Grunde nicht mit der von Mitch verkörperten Realität vereinbar. Die Schülerinnen und Schüler sollten zu folgenden Ergebnissen kommen:

- since marriage connotes happiness, protection and fulfilment, Mitch's marriage proposal provokes a very emotional response from Blanche
- it is probably a quite abstract thought of marital bliss that fires Blanche's enthusiasm
- it is apparently not the prospect of marrying Mitch, the man himself, that makes Blanche go into raptures, but the function that this man might fulfil; for a moment, Mitch seems to be the *deus ex machina* that has appeared suddenly and unexpectedly in order to provide a solution to her apparently insoluble difficulties

Die Ernüchterung, Enttäuschung und Verzweiflung Blanches angesichts Mitchs Nichterscheinen auf ihrer Geburtstagsfeier sowie die Ursachen und Begleitumstände dieses Umstandes sollen von den Schülerinnen und Schülern im Rahmen einer Hausaufgabe resümiert bzw. analysiert werden. Da Stanleys Handeln ausschlaggebend ist für die Demütigungen, Beleidigungen und Verletzungen, denen Blanche insbesondere in Szene 8 ausgesetzt ist, erscheint es sinnvoll zu sein, die Aufmerksamkeit der Lerngruppe auf dessen Gebaren in den Szenen 7 und 8 zu lenken. Somit ergehen folgende Arbeitsaufträge an die Schülerinnen und Schüler:

1. Summarize scenes 7 und 8.
2. Analyse und interpret the quotations on the worksheet *(Copy 7)*.

Quotations (scenes 7 and 8)

1. STANLEY: "And you run out an' get her cokes, I suppose? And serve 'em to her Majesty in the tub?" (p. 105, ll. 20, 21)

2. STANLEY: "That girl calls *me* common." (p. 106, l. 5)

3. STANLEY: "But even the management of the Flamingo was impressed by Dame Blanche! In fact they were so impressed by Dame Blanche that they requested her to turn in her room-key – for permanently!" (p. 108, ll. 2–6)

4. STANLEY: "Boy, oh, boy, I'd like to have been in that office when Dame Blanche was called on the carpet. I'd like to have seen her trying to squirm out of that one." (p. 110, ll. 20–23)

5. STANLEY: "You're goddam right I told him! I'd have that on my conscience the rest of my life if I knew all that stuff und let my best friend get caught!" (p. 113, ll. 10–12)

6. STELLA: "What'll – she – do? What on earth will she – do!"
   STANLEY: "Her future is mapped out for her."
   STELLA: "What do you mean?" (p. 114, ll. 14–17)

7. STANLEY: "Don't ever talk that way to me! *Pig – Polack – disgusting – vulgar – greasy!* – them kind of words have been on your tongue und your sister's too much around here! What do you think you two are? A pair of queens? Remember what Huey Long said – *Every Man is a King!* And I am the king around here, so don't forget it!" (p. 118, ll. 20–26)

8. BLANCHE: "You healthy Polack, without a nerve in your body, of course you don't know what anxiety feels like!"
   Stanley: "I am not a Polack. People from Poland are Poles, not Polacks. But what I am is a one hundred per cent American, born and raised in the greatest country on earth and proud as hell of it, so don't ever call me a Polack." (p. 121, ll. 8–15)

9. STANLEY: "I pulled you down off them columns and how you loved it, having them coloured lights going! And wasn't we happy together, wasn't it all okay till she showed here?" (p. 123, ll. 22–25)

Humiliation, violation and dignity

3.1 Revelations and reactions (scenes 7 and 8)

Der sich in den vorangegangenen Szenen manifestierende und von subtilen Machtspielen begleitete Konflikt zwischen Blanche und Stanley kulminiert in Szene 8 in offen zur Schau gestelltem Hass. Sowohl die von Stanley mit abgrundtiefer Boshaftigkeit und giftigem Zynismus initiierte Überreichung von Busrückfahrkarten an Blanche als auch das von Blanche in Stanleys Gegenwart gebrauchte Wort *Polack* sind Indikatoren für die Unvereinbarkeit und Unversöhnlichkeit der von den beiden Protagonisten repräsentierten Anschauungen. Da neben dem die Szenen 7 und 8 dominierenden Klassenantagonismus auch die Argumente bzw. Rechtfertigungen, welche der von Stella ob seiner Grobheit und Rücksichtslosigkeit gegenüber Blanche gescholtene und teilweise in die Enge getriebene Stanley für sein Handeln ins Feld führt, von zentraler Bedeutung sind, sollten die Schülerinnen und Schüler nach der Präsentation der von ihnen angefertigten Zusammenfassungen und Interpretationen in die Lage versetzt werden, Stanleys Motive, Argumente sowie Beschwichtigungsversuche einer genauen Analyse sowie einer umfassenden Bewertung zu unterziehen. Der der Bewertung bzw. Kommentierung von Stanleys Beweggründen bzw. Motiven zwangsläufig anhaftende spekulative Charakter soll im Übrigen dazu genutzt werden, den Schülerinnen und Schülern diverse Kreativaufgaben zu stellen, welche ihnen eine umfassende bzw. subtile Sichtweise auf Stanleys Handeln ermöglichen.

Die von den Schülerinnen und Schülern im Rahmen der Hausaufgabe verfassten Zusammenfassungen der Szenen 7 und 8 sowie die von ihnen vorgenommenen Interpretationen könnten folgende Gestalt angenommen haben:

It is Blanche's birthday. While Stella is preparing Blanche's birthday dinner, Stanley arrives on the scene und starts inquiring about Blanche's whereabouts. On hearing that she is in the bathroom, he starts making sarcastic comments about Blanche's constant cleansing rituals. Insinuating that she might desire to be cleansed of her sins, he sets about giving Stella compromising details about Blanche's promiscuous behaviour in Laurel and the loss of her teaching post for seducing one of her young students. Although Stella refuses to accept Stanley's assertions as true, she has to admit that Blanche's flightiness used to cause her parents a great deal of anxiety. Since Stella knows about her sister's sensitivity and the disastrous effect that her husband's suicide has had on her, she is appalled to learn that Stanley has informed Mitch about Blanche's past, thus destroying her hopes of getting re-married. When Blanche leaves the bathroom, she seems to have a hunch that something is wrong.

After finishing the birthday meal that has taken place in the absence of Mitch, Blanche desperately tries to maintain a shred of dignity by pretending to be light-hearted and amusing. Ignoring Blanche's attempts at making conversation and resenting his wife's criticism of his table manners, Stanley flies into a rage and hurls cups und saucers to the floor. After having talked to one of his buddies on the phone, he gives Blanche his birthday present: a bus ticket back to Laurel. Unable to cope with Stanley's cruelty and cynicism, Blanche jumps up from the table, heads for the toilet und starts being sick. Stella's ensuing diatribe against her husband's rudeness and cruelty is interrupted by the onset of labour pains. She has to be taken to a hospital.

Lösungsvorschlag zu *Copy 7*

1. By sneering at Stella's complete submission to her sister's wishes and referring to Blanche as "Her Majesty", he makes it clear that he loathes Blanche's air of superiority, her odd habits, her mannerisms, her affectation and the influence she has over her sister.

2. Although the adjective *common* is very often used as a synonym of *ordinary* or *average,* it is apparent that Stanley ascribes a different meaning to it. To him it is a derogative term that is synonymous with adjectives like *vulgar* and *uneducated.* Since he sees himself as a hard-working, law-abiding and well-respected member of society, he finds it unbearable that a woman with a bad reputation who lacks a job, a family and money should look down on him.

3. The tone of Stanley's description is mocking and his words savour of triumphalism as well as malicious glee. He is apparently pleased about Blanche's humiliation. By referring to her as "Dame Blanche", he emphasizes the gap between the *Imaginary* and the *Actual* in Blanche's life. Though giving herself airs, she is little more than a mere prostitute.

4. Once again, Stanley makes plain that he delights in the revelation of Blanche's offences und transgressions.

5. Since Stella scolds him for his cruelty to Blanche, he tries to justify his behaviour. Claiming that his revelations have been to the benefit of his friend Mitch, he intends to make it clear that he has acted on moral grounds.

6. Stanley gives the impression of being fully aware of the horrible consequences Blanche will have to face if she is turned out by him. His straightforward remark reveals that he regards Blanche's impending personal catastrophe as a law of nature: Those who cannot meet society's demands are bound to end up in misery – it's as simple as that. In this particular context, it is worth noting that Stella's desperation in the face of her sister's misery does not affect him at all.

7. Stanley's getting worked up about Stella's criticism of his table manners reveals him not only to be generally sensitive to criticism but to be particularly sensitive about his ethnic origins and his identity. His quoting of Huey Long, on the other hand, is indicative of his marked class consciousness und his approval of socialistic ideas.

8. Blanche und Stanley's heated exchange epitomizes their vast different outlooks and values. Blanche's class snobbery, which makes her label Stanley as a *healthy Polack* is in sharp contrast to Stanley's patriotism and allegiance to the United States of America. Since he obviously believes in American values and ideals, his outlook is based on the assumption that classes are non-existent and that there is equality of opportunity. Blanche, however, embodies Southern aristocracy and associates both Stanley's healthy body and his simplicity with a lack of sensitivity and education.

9. Stanley wants Stella to realize that she belongs to him. He wants to remind Stella of her relief at having escaped the decadence of her parental home, and what is more, he wants her to comprehend that it is Blanche who is to blame for the troubles and arguments that are characterizing their marriage at the moment.

Die im Zuge der Interpretation diverser Aussagen bzw. Aussprüche Stanleys sowie der Schwestern Blanche und Stella hervorgebrachten Ergebnisse sollen im Folgenden dazu genutzt werden, die Schülerinnen und Schüler in die Lage zu versetzen, die Motive und Gründe zu erörtern, welche Stanley dazu bewegt haben mögen, seine Kenntnisse über Blanches Vergangenheit zu nutzen, um sie zu diskreditieren bzw. zu demütigen. Dieses Vorgehen bietet sich nicht nur deshalb an, weil das Auswerten bzw. Bewerten von Ergebnissen in der wissenschaftspropädeutischen Ausbildung eine wichtige Rolle spielt, sondern ist zudem vor dem Hintergrund der in Szene 10 erfolgenden Vergewaltigung Blanches von entscheidender Bedeutung. Um den Schülerinnen und Schülern zu verdeutlichen, wie weit das Spektrum von Motiven und Beweggründen ist, welche ein Mensch haben kann, um sich veranlasst zu sehen, einen Mitmenschen zu diskreditieren bzw. zu demütigen, werden sie zunächst aufgefordert, allgemeine, ihnen bekannte Motive zu benennen. Somit ergeht folgender Arbeitsauftrag an die Lerngruppe:

Generally speaking, what can lead people to denigrate and humiliate others?

Die von den Schülerinnen und Schülern genannten Begriffe bzw. Stichworte werden zwecks späterer Auswertung an der Tafel gesammelt.

- vengeance
- jealousy
- class hatred
- sadism
- malice
- malicious glee
- injured pride
- someone is engaged in a power struggle

- to be power-mad
- a show of strength/force
- a strategy to impose one's will on other people
- frustration
- someone feels slighted
- somebody's character has a mean streak

Die von den Schülerinnen und Schülern genannten Motive sowie Beweggründe sollen in einem nächsten Unterrichtsschritt hinsichtlich ihrer Tauglichkeit als mögliche Erklärungen für Stanleys Verhalten untersucht werden. Deshalb sollen sie sich im Rahmen einer kurzen Partnerarbeit folgender Aufgabenstellung widmen:

Look at the motives listed on the board and decide which of these motives might account for Stanley's behaviour. Give reasons.

In Anlehnung an die im Rahmen der Hausaufgabe erfolgten Interpretationen *(Copy 6)* wären folgende Schülerbeiträge denkbar:

- Stanley is <u>jealous</u> of Blanche because she is the focus of Mitch und Stella's attention. He <u>feels slighted</u>.
- He might feel a pang of <u>jealousy</u> because Blanche feels attracted to Mitch and not to him.
- Since Blanche tends to tease him about his lack of education and his origin, his <u>pride is hurt</u>.
- Having overheard Blanche's condemnations of him, Stanley aims at <u>taking revenge on her.</u>
- Regarding himself as the "cock of the walk", he is used to imposing his will on other people: Since Stella and particularly Blanche start opposing him, he thinks it necessary to make a show of strength/force.
- Since his character apparently has a <u>mean streak</u> (he hits his wife and bosses about his friends), his actions might be traced back to <u>sheer malice</u>.
- Being very class conscious and suspicious of the irresponsible aristocracy, his actions might have been driven by <u>class-hatred</u>.

Angesichts der in Szene 9 vonstattengehenden versuchten Vergewaltigung Blanches durch Mitch und der in Szene 10 schließlich brutal durchgeführten Schändung Blanches durch Stanley, ist es von großer Wichtigkeit, die Schülerinnen und Schüler im Vorfeld der Besprechung der genannten Szenen für Stanleys sowie Mitchs Gemütslage zu sensibilisieren. Im Rückgriff auf die Erklärungsversuche, die hinsichtlich Stanleys Verhalten gegenüber Blanche unternommen worden sind und in Anlehnung an die Einzelheiten, die über Mitchs Persönlichkeit zu Tage gefördert worden sind (siehe 2.3.), erstellen die Schülerinnen und Schüler in der Folge einen Dialog, welcher das Gespräch, in dem Stanley Mitch über Blanches Verfehlungen und zwielichtigen Ruf aufklärt, nachzeichnet. Das Erstellen des angesprochenen Dialogs wird durch folgenden Arbeitsauftrag eingeleitet:

Imagine Williams' drama contains a scene in which Stanley informs Mitch about Blanche's promiscuous behaviour. What might the conversation between the two men have been like? Write a dialogue in which you draw on the knowledge you have acquired of Stanley's as well as Mitch's personality.

Die anschließende Präsentation der Dialoge wird mit folgender *while-listening activity* begleitet:

Listen to your classmates' dialogues and say to what extent they reflect Stanley's/Mitch's character/state of mind.

In Vorbereitung auf die Demütigungen, denen Blanche in den Szenen 9 und 10 unter anderem durch eine Vergewaltigung bzw. einen Vergewaltigungsversuch ausgesetzt ist, lesen die Schülerinnen und Schüler die genannten Szenen im Rahmen einer Hausaufgabe unter folgenden Aufgabenstellungen:

1. Read scenes 9 and 10. Find a quote or a stage direction that epitomizes the respective scenes and thus might serve as an adequate title.

2. Comment on the differences between Blanche's behaviour towards Mitch and her behaviour towards Stanley.

3.2 Booze, rape and the start of Blanche's disintegration (scenes 9 and 10)

Obschon die sich in Szene 9 andeutende Katastrophe (versuchte Vergewaltigung Blanches) und die in Szene 10 einsetzende Katastrophe (Vergewaltigung Blanches) von einer augenfälligen äußeren Handlung (Hilfeschreie, gewaltsames Entfernen einer Papierlaterne, Zerbrechen eines Spiegels, hektisches Telefonieren, Zerschlagen einer Flasche etc.) eingerahmt ist, darf nicht übersehen werden, dass es sich hierbei um verzichtbare dramatische Effekte handelt, die bei der durch die Schülerinnen und Schüler vorgenommenen Auswahl emblematischer Passagen bzw. Zitate nur eine untergeordnete Rolle spielen sollten. Den Schülerinnen und Schülern sollte beim Anfertigen der Hausaufgabe aufgefallen sein, dass Blanche neben der Einsicht in die Unentrinnbarkeit ihres Schicksals auch die Fähigkeit zur Introspektion besitzt. Ihre Vorahnung, dass das Zusammentreffen mit Stanley in einer Katastrophe enden wird, legt hiervon genauso eindeutig Zeugnis ab wie ihre gegenüber Mitch abgegebenen, schon fast dialektischen Charakter tragenden Erklärungen, welche dieser ironischerweise nicht versteht. Somit könnten die Schülerinnen und Schüler bei einer sorgfältigen Erledigung des ersten Teils der Hausaufgabe zu folgenden Ergebnissen gekommen sein:

> A quote that epitomizes scene 9: BLANCHE: **"I've never lied in my heart."**
> Reason for choice:
> Blanche's capacity for introspection, which enables her to unequivocally tell the truth about herself, is not appreciated by Mitch. The subtle analysis that Blanche presents of her current and past behaviour is not only beyond Mitch's grasp, but also arouses his anger. Since he can only comprehend that Blanche has had a lot of affairs, but is not able to grasp the motives behind her behaviour, he has the feeling of having been fooled.
>
> A quote that epitomizes scene 10: STANLEY: **"We've had this date with each other from the beginning!"**
>
> Reason for choice:
> In spite of being drunk and almost out of her mind, Blanche is put on her guard when she realizes that she is alone with Stanley. Without being threatened or bullied, she gives the impression of being cornered and harassed. Ironically, it is her very effort to keep up her dignity and her attempt to prevent Stanley from doing her harm that goad him into attacking her verbally and physically. Thus, the rape of Blanche is not so much the result of Stanley's outrage and sexual arousal as a symbol of the inevitability of Blanche's destiny. Right from the beginning of the drama, she is in the grip of some strong and invincible power that makes her inevitably head for destruction.

Hinsichtlich der Untersuchung der Unterschiede, welches Blanches Verhalten gegenüber Mitch (Szene 9) und Stanley (Szene 10) aufweist, könnten die Schülerinnen und Schüler zu folgenden Resultaten gekommen sein:

Blanche's behaviour in scene 9:
- although she is drunk, she is able to confront Mitch without losing her self-control
- she is guileless, that is to say, she does not suspect Mitch of setting out to rape her
- she is honest insofar as she unequivocally tells the truth about her past
- she is introspective inasmuch as she analyses and explains the reasons for her behaviour in the past
- although Mitch is apparently drunk and difficult to deal with, Blanche is able to rise to the occasion/challenge

Blanche's behaviour in scene 10:
- she is deeply suspicious of Stanley (the conversation with Mitch has obviously put a strain on her)
- she is on edge
- she is hostile towards Stanley
- she puts on airs and pretends to have an appointment with the millionaire Shep Huntleigh
- she is haunted by feelings of insecurity and cannot rise to the occasion

Da das Verhalten Blanches in den Szenen 9 und 10 neben entscheidenden Unterschieden auch Konstanten aufweist, die in engem Zusammenhang mit ihrer charakterlichen Disposition stehen, werden die Schülerinnen und Schüler nach der Präsentation der Hausaufgabe mit folgendem Arbeitsauftrag betraut:

Skim through pages 125–146 and find out whether there are similarities between Blanche's behaviour in scenes 9 and 10.

Die zu erwartenden Resultate werden zwecks späterer Analyse an der Tafel festgehalten:

Similarities:
- her lack of awareness of the effects her words and behaviour might have on Mitch and Stanley
- her conduct and manners that are odd enough to immediately create a distance between herself and the two men
- her horror and disgust of proletarian roughness and cruelty
- her desperate attempts to escape from the menacing situations she has got herself in
- her acknowledgement that she has made a lot of mistakes, and what is more, her admission to a sense of guilt

Angesichts der schon benannten Korrelation zwischen Blanches Verhalten in den Szenen 9 und 10 und ihrer charakterlichen Disposition sollen die Schülerinnen und Schüler in einem nächsten Unterrichtsschritt unter Rückgriff auf die erarbeiteten Gemeinsamkeiten sowie Unterschiede, die Blanches Verhalten in den genannten Szenen aufweist, eine Diskussion über ihre Persönlichkeitsstruktur führen. Dieser didaktische Ansatz scheint nicht nur im Hinblick auf das Einüben von Debatiertechniken sinnvoll zu sein, sondern kann darüber hinaus auch als eine umfassende und hilfreiche Grundlage für eine zum Abschluss der Dramenbesprechung zu erstellende Charakterisierung Blanches dienen. Demnach ergeht folgender Arbeitsauftrag an die Lerngruppe:

> Discuss the following statement: Blanche's behaviour throughout the drama reveals her to be a split personality; particularly scenes 9 and 10 give evidence of her highly volatile disposition.

Bevor sich die Schülerinnen und Schüler in Gruppen von jeweils drei Personen auf die Debatte vorbereiten, werden zunächst im Plenum Argumente gesammelt, welche die oben aufgeführte Aussage stützen bzw. entkräften. Um den Schülerinnen und Schülern das Vertreten ihres jeweiligen Standpunktes in den Gruppen zu erleichtern, werden die im Plenum genannten Argumente an der Tafel aufgelistet:

Arguments in favour of the statement:

- although wilfully pretending to be oblivious to the causes of the loss of Belle Reve, in reality she knows that the family's financial ruin can be traced back to extravagance and debauchery
- Blanche's actions are unpredictable (she smashes mirrors, dresses up in fancy clothes, etc.)
- her behaviour is characterized by severe mood swings
- on the one hand, Blanche is very perceptive, but on the other hand, she is completely oblivious to the effect that her behaviour has on her surroundings
- although having an intuitive awareness of Stanley's dangerousness, she provokes him by showing a sense of superiority
- in spite of setting great store by education and sophistication, she wants to marry an uneducated man like Mitch

Arguments against the statement:

- she is continually self-absorbed
- she always tries to give the impression of being a dignified person
- Blanche's propensity for giving herself airs never changes
- even though she at times gives the impression of brimming with self-confidence and cheerfulness, there is always an undercurrent of despair in her manner
- although Blanche at times gives the impression of being oblivious to her surroundings she is very perceptive; her obliviousness is not due to a lack of perceptiveness, but can only be traced back to a lack of interest in uneducated people

---

Um die Schülerinnen und Schüler für die Gründe zu sensibilisieren, die dazu führen, dass Blanche einem Vergewaltigungsversuch durch Mitch und einer Vergewaltigung durch Stanley ausgesetzt ist, werden sie abschließend aufgefordert, Dialoge zwischen Blanche und den beiden Männern zu erstellen, die friedvoll bzw. gewaltfrei ausklingen. Da es in diesem Zusammenhang von zentraler Wichtigkeit ist, dass die Schülerinnen und Schüler neben Mitchs Provinzialität und engem Moralkodex auch Stanleys Klassenbewusstsein und Triebhaftigkeit in ihre Überlegungen einbeziehen, wird diesem Umstand bei der Formulierung der an die Jungen und Mädchen des Kurses ergehenden Arbeitsaufträge Rechnung getragen:

> Boys: imagine you are Tennessee Williams and you have to rewrite scene 9. Make up a dialogue between Mitch and Blanche that does not culmi-

nate in Mitch's attempt to rape Blanche. Make sure that the course of their conversation makes it appear logical that Mitch is not goaded into harassing Blanche. Pay special attention to Mitch's narrow-mindedness, his strict moral code and his lack of education.

Girls: imagine you are Tennessee Williams and you have to rewrite scene 10. Make up a dialogue between Stanley and Blanche that does not culminate in Stanley's raping Blanche. Make sure that the course of their conversation makes it appear logical that Stanley is not goaded into raping Blanche. Pay special attention to Stanley's class consciousness, his pride, his intuition and his animalism.

In Anbetracht der Tatsache, dass das zentrale Ereignis in Szene 11, nämlich die anstehende Überweisung Blanches in eine Nervenheilanstalt, nicht nur von melodramatischen Effekten begleitet wird, sondern sich darüber hinaus dem Leser bzw. Zuschauer erst nach und nach erschließt, ist es für die Schaffung einer angemessenen Diskussionsgrundlage von entscheidender Bedeutung, dass die Schülerinnen und Schüler in die Lage versetzt werden, sowohl die anstehende Einlieferung Blanches als auch die ihr zugrunde liegenden Kausalitäten zu erkennen bzw. einzuordnen. Um dieses zu gewährleisten, wird der Lerngruppe im Rahmen einer Hausaufgabe ein Arbeitsblatt mit Satzfragmenten (*Copy 8*) an die Hand gegeben, deren korrekte Vervollständigung voraussetzt, dass Szene 11 genauestens gelesen und verstanden worden ist. Mit dem Ziel, eine fruchtbare Diskussion hinsichtlich der Wichtigkeit des auf den ersten Blick Plakativen bzw. Vordergründigen in Williams Drama zu initiieren, setzen sich die Schülerinnen und Schüler darüber hinaus mit den Begriffen *melodrama* und *melodramatic* auseinander. Somit ergehen folgende Arbeitsaufträge an die Lerngruppe:

1. Complete the sentences on the worksheet (Copy 8).

2. Look up the terms *melodrama* and *melodramatic* and decide to what extent they apply to scene 11.

3.3 Committal to a mental hospital

Die von den Schülerinnen und Schülern präsentierte Hausaufgabe (siehe 3.2) soll im Folgenden als Grundlage für die Diskussion bzw. Untersuchung der in Szene 11 manifest werdenden inneren Konflikte sowie melodramatischen Ereignisse dienen. Es ist zu erwarten, dass die Lerngruppe beim Anfertigen der Hausaufgabe zu folgenden Ergebnissen gekommen ist:

Lösungsvorschlag zu *Copy 8*:

1. ... they want to prevent her from becoming agitated.
2. ... reminds her of having been raped by Stanley.
3. ... would have found out about Stella and Eunice's plan before the doctors arrived.
4. ... would have sued Stanley for raping her.
5. ... is to go on living with Stanley ...
6. ... would show more consideration for Blanche.
7. ... it dawns upon him that he and Stanley are to blame for the humiliation and unfair treatment that Blanche has been subjected to.
8. ... Stella is extremely guilt-ridden and is about to have a nervous breakdown.

Scene 11

1. Eunice and Stella show deep concern for Blanche's physical and emotional well-being because ...

_____

_____

_____

2. Blanche starts panicking when she hears Stanley's voice because it ...

_____

_____

_____

3. If Blanche had not been so vain and self-absorbed, she ...

_____

_____

_____

4. If Blanche had had more get-up and strength, she ...

_____

_____

_____

5. If Stella _____,
   she must believe that the story of the rape is the invention of a mentally unstable woman.

6. If Stanley had a guilty conscience, he ...

_____

_____

_____

7. Mitch is dejected and irritable because ...

_____

_____

_____

8. Eunice is very concerned about Stella's mental well-being because ...

_____

_____

_____

9. On leaving her sister's flat, Blanche does not turn around because ...

_____

_____

_____

10. If Stella did not feel so attracted to Stanley, ...

_____

_____

_____

9. ... she probably wants to indicate that it is beneath her dignity to show regard for the people that have deceived her. She might also want to signal that she has found a safe haven and is no longer dependent on her sister's help and support.
10. ... she would not sacrifice her sister's well-being for sexual gratification.

Im Rahmen der Bearbeitung von Aufgabenteil 2 ist mit folgendem Resultat zu rechnen:

The word melodramatic is a pejorative term that is often applied to plays that are characterized by sensational plots, violent incidents and over-simplified characterizations of heroes and villains.

Da die in Williams Drama verankerten melodramatischen Elemente jedoch keineswegs als bloße Effekthascherei abgetan werden können, sondern in der Mehrzahl der Fälle eine symbolische Funktion erfüllen, sollte die Aufmerksamkeit der Lerngruppe auf diesen Umstand gelenkt werden. Um die Schülerinnen und Schüler zur Reflexion über die Funktion diverser Ereignisse anzuregen, wird ihnen ein Arbeitsblatt ausgehändigt, auf dem melodramatische Ereignisse aus Szene 11 und anderen Szenen des Dramas aufgelistet sind. Die Aufgabe der Schülerinnen und Schüler besteht nunmehr darin, die Funktion der aufgelisteten Ereignisse zu ermitteln:

Comment on the deeper meaning of the incidents listed on the worksheet (Copy 9).

Various incidents and their deeper meaning

1. Blanche arriving at her sister's place in a *rattle-trap streetcar named Desire.* (scene 1)

_____

_____

_____

2. Stanley's drunken rage that makes him beat up his wife. (scene 3)

_____

_____

_____

3. Blanche revealing her husband's suicide and its causes. (scene 6)

_____

_____

_____

4. Stanley hurling cups and saucers to the floor. (scene 8)

_____

_____

_____

5. Mitch's attempted rape of Blanche. (scene 9)

_____

_____

_____

6. Blanche slamming her hand mirror face down with such violence that the glass cracks. (scene 10)

_____

_____

_____

7. Stanley raping Blanche. (scene 10)

_____

_____

_____

8. Mitch lunging at and striking Stanley. (scene 11)

_____

_____

_____

9. Stanley tearing the paper lantern from the light bulb. (scene 11)

_____

_____

_____

10. Blanche struggling with the Matron. (scene 11)

_____

_____

_____

Folgende symbolische Bedeutungen sollten die Schülerinnen den aufgelisteten Ereignissen beimessen:

Lösungsvorschlag zu *Copy 9*:

1. "A streetcar named Desire" that is heading for "Cemeteries" is not just a symbol of the inevitability and inexorability of Blanche's fate, but also reflects the tragic course of her existence. Having been driven by a frantic sexual passion throughout her life, she finally ends up in a mental hospital, a place that symbolizes the burial of all hopes and dreams of fulfilment and happiness.
2. This particular incident stresses Stanley's dangerousness and his will to dominate his surroundings.
3. Blanche's revelation gives the reader/spectator an insight into the reasons for her being in a constant state of agitation and anxiety.
4. This particular outburst is supposed to lay emphasis on the fact that Stanley is very proud and extremely sensitive about his origins.
5. Mitch's "unsuccessful" attempt to rape Blanche illustrates that he lacks strength, get-up and will power.
6. Blanche's smashing the mirror is indicative of her desperation and torment in the face of her fading beauty.
7. The rape perpetrated by Stanley is symptomatic of his fierce animalistic instincts. As soon as something or someone stirs him up and he senses weakness or cowardice, he swoops down on his prey.
8. Mitch's ridiculously feeble and ineffectual attempt to square up to Stanley is not only indicative of his impotent outrage at the harsh treatment of Blanche, but also shows his ineffectiveness and inability to stand his ground.
9. Tearing the paper lantern from the light bulb not only exposes Blanche to the glaring light, but in a figurative sense also lays bare her blighted life and her shame. Stanley's action might also remind Blanche of his stripping her of her clothes during the rape.
10. Blanche's futile attempt to free herself from the Matron's firm grasp symbolizes the inevitability of her fate.

Um die Untersuchung hinsichtlich des Einsatzes melodramatischer Elemente in Williams Drama und die damit verbundene Sympathielenkung zu vertiefen, diskutieren die Schülerinnen und Schüler in einem nächsten Unterrichtsschritt folgende Fragestellung im Plenum:

What might make the reader sympathize with Blanche after reading scene 11?

Von den Schülerinnen und Schülern möglicherweise hervorgebrachte Äußerungen wie z. B. „the humiliations she has been exposed to" oder „although she has been humiliated, she maintains her dignity" sollen schließlich als Grundlage für die Bearbeitung einer Kreativaufgabe dienen, die es der Lerngruppe ermöglicht, das menschliche Versagen der für die Einlieferung Blanches in eine Nervenheilanstalt verantwortlichen Personen zu spezifizieren. Somit ergeht folgender Arbeitsauftrag an die Schülerinnen und Schüler:

Imagine that Shep Huntleigh, Blanche's former beau, has been informed about the humiliations Blanche has had to suffer at her sister's place. He decides to set out on a journey to Elysian Fields in order to give Stella,

> Eunice, Mitch und Stanley a piece of his mind. Make up a monologue that comprises the things that he would probably tell the above mentioned people on his arrival. Make sure you use stage directions that reflect Shep's inner turmoil.

Eine von den Schülerinnen und Schülern verfasste, an Stanley gerichtete Diatribe könnte folgende Gestalt annehmen:

> (Shep enters the kitchen und has to thread his way through a maze of chairs. He stops right in front of Blanche's former bed and screws up his face against the glaring light bulb hanging from the ceiling.)
>
> SHEP: "So this is the place where Blanche had to live off the crumbs from your table, the place that marked the beginning of her end. Oh, it's such a shame that an educated and sophisticated woman like her had to be put through this horrible experience. She used to be so entertaining, sweet-spirited and witty, but I guess (pointing at Stanley) witticisms of which you are not the author are hardly to your taste. Bossing people about, cracking jokes at their expense and abusing them physically when they give you a piece of their mind is all you can do. Do you know what you are? (He gives Stanley a hostile glare) No? Let me tell you what you are? You are a selfish criminal who has no consideration for others, a cowardly rapist who is not able to control his perverse sex drive, and on top of that, an incredibly pathetic brute who is guilty of deliberate cruelty. It is your jealousy of people who are more educated than you und your gigantic inferiority complex that impelled you to intimidate, abuse, violate and slander a woman that is superior to you in every respect. (Shouting) Get out of my sight, you pathetic and malicious wretch or I'll kill you.

Die Tatsache, dass Blanche im Gegensatz zu ihrer Schwester Stella am Ende des Dramas durch subtile Sympathielenkung zu einer Art moralischen Siegerin mutiert, soll Anlass dazu gehen, die Schülerinnen und Schüler im Rahmen einer Hausaufgabe folgende Aussage kommentieren zu lassen:

> In scene 11, Blanche wins a great moral victory. Stella, by contrast, proves to be a deceitful and callous nymphomaniac who has sold out her sister for sexual gratification.

Der von den Schülerinnen und Schülern verfasste Kommentar könnte folgende Gesichtspunkte umfassen:

> Although Blanche has neither done harm to Stanley nor to Stella, she is victimized twice:
> * Stanley rapes her
> * Stella deceives her by committing her to a mental hospital
>
> Leaving on the doctor's arm without a backward glance, Blanche finally assumes the dignity she has been deprived of earlier on. While her detractor Stanley und her sister Stella are left behind with their tail between their legs, she seems to rise above her degradation and arouses sympathy and admiration in the audience. Thus, she wins a moral victory.

At first glance, it seems to be justified to call Stella deceitful und callous because
- she is not frank with Blanche about what she has planned
- committing Blanche to a mental hospital means destroying her life
- committing her sister to a mental hospital is meant to conceal the crime that has been committed by the man she is sexually attracted to

To call Stella callous might be out of place because
- she feels sympathy for her sister
- she has a guilty conscience
- she is desperate
- she would have liked to help her sister

Um eine intensive Auseinandersetzung mit den quälenden Gewissenskonflikten, denen Stella und Mitch ausgesetzt sind, zu gewährleisten, wäre es alternativ auch denkbar, einen Teil der Lerngruppe dazu zu veranlassen, einen Tagebucheintrag im Namen von Stella oder Mitch zu verfassen, in dem schon herausgearbeitete Eigenschaften und Beweggründe der beiden (siehe *Copy 7/Copy 8*) im Sinne eines Transfers zum Tragen kommen sollten. Die hierauf basierende Aufgabenstellung könnte wie folgt lauten:

Imagine you are Mitch/Stella. After Blanche has been committed to a mental hospital, you write your thoughts in your diary.

Die von den Schülerinnen und Schülern verfassten Tagebucheinträge könnten folgende Aspekte umfassen:

Stella:
- she admits that she is responsible for her sister's fall from grace
- she blames herself for her dishonesty
- she plans to make up for her despicable behaviour towards her sister
- she complains about being a slave to the bondage of a sexually-attractive husband, etc.

Mitch:
- he blames Stanley for mistreating Blanche
- he swears to break off his friendship with Stanley
- he blames himself for being narrow-minded, cowardly and callous
- he blames himself for not having stood up for Blanche
- he plans to make up for his lack of courage and empathy by visiting Blanche und trying to support her, etc.

Film Analysis

Die folgenden Unterrichtssequenzen konzentrieren sich neben einer kurzen Diskussion über die Machbarkeit bzw. Zweckmäßigkeit einer filmischen Umsetzung von Williams' Drama im Wesentlichen auf die Gegenüberstellung des Originaldramas mit dem 1951 unter der Regie von Elia Kazan entstandenen Kinofilm. Obschon neuere bzw. aktuellere filmische Umsetzungen des Dramas *A Streetcar Named Desire* existieren, erweist sich eine nähere Untersuchung von Kazans Film nicht nur aufgrund der herausragenden schauspielerischen Leistungen von Marlon Brando, Vivien Leigh und Karl Malden als sinnvoll, sondern vor allem aufgrund der teils augenfälligen teils subtilen Unterschiede, welche die Filmversion gegenüber dem Originaldrama aufweist. Das Aufdecken bzw. die Analyse der filmischen Abweichungen versetzt die Schülerinnen und Schüler nicht nur in die Lage, ihr im Verlaufe der Dramenbesprechung erlangtes Wissen hinsichtlich des Handlungsverlaufs, der Charaktere und der alles durchdringenden Symbolik anzuwenden bzw. zu vertiefen, sondern sie werden darüber hinaus auch mit den für die genannten Abweichungen ursächlichen künstlerischen sowie gesellschaftspolitischen Hintergründen vertraut gemacht.

Die im Rahmen der Filmanalyse gemachten Zeit- und Szenenangaben beziehen sich allesamt auf die deutsche Fassung der 2006 bei Warner Brothers erschienenen DVD *Endstation Sehnsucht* (Special Edition 2–Disc Set). Die Bestellnummer lautet: 7 321921 389320. Die DVD bietet neben der Möglichkeit, den Film in der Originalsprache Englisch zu schauen, auch die Möglichkeit, englische Untertitel einzublenden.

Die im Folgenden erstellte Szenenübersicht deckt sich weitestgehend mit der Szeneneinteilung, die auf der oben erwähnten DVD vorgenommen wird.

Opening credits	The front of the shabby corner house in which Stella and Stanley live is shown.	0:00–1:12
Scene 1	Blanche arrives at New Orleans central station and sets off for Elysian Fields in a streetcar named Desire. Having arrived at Elysian Fields, she is very surprised at the rundown quality of her sister's house.	1:13–3:50
Scene 2	Blanche and Stella's reunion takes place in a bowling alley where Stanley and his friends are about to kick off a row. Feeling very tired and unattractive, Blanche refuses to be introduced to Stanley. Consequently, the two sisters continue their conversation in a nearby restaurant. There is an undercurrent of tension in their meeting.	3:51–7:02
Scene 3	Having arrived at the Kowalski apartment, Stella starts raving to Blanche about Stanley. Blanche, on the other hand, informs Stella about the loss of Belle Reve. In a fit of hysteria, she accuses Stella of having let her down.	7:03–10:56
Scene 4	Stanley arrives at Elysian Fields. There is an uneasy meeting between him and Blanche. In the course of their conversation, Blanche is reminded of her dead husband and almost breaks down.	10:57–14:19
Scene 5	Stella informs Stanley about the loss of Belle Reve. Wanting to know how the mansion was lost and being under the impression that Stella is trying to fob him off with excuses, Stanley works himself into a frenzy. Furious, he pulls open Blanche's large trunk and displays all her finery, which he believes to be genuine.	14:20–19:35

Scene 6	While dolling herself up for a night out, Blanche flirts with Stanley. Instead of paying her the compliments she expects, he demands to see the papers relating to the sale of Belle Reve and pulls open Blanche's trunk to look for them. To Blanche's distress, he finds the letters of her dead husband. Stanley justifies his inquisitiveness by telling Blanche that he has to look after his wife's interests. In this connection, he reveals that Stella is expecting a baby. When Stella finally arrives, Blanche congratulates her on her pregnancy.	19:36–28:20
Scene 7	Stanley's friends arrive at Elysian Fields to play poker. Blanche and Stella have enjoyed a night out at the theatre and return to Elysian Fields. The poker game is still going on, but after a while, Mitch refuses to go on playing.	28:21–32:53
Scene 8	In spite of Stanley's intermittent protests, Mitch is having a conversation with Blanche in her bedroom.	32:54–36:42
Scene 9	Stanley is very drunk and resentful of Mitch's interest in Blanche. To give vent to his pent-up anger, he throws Stella's radio out of the window. Stella starts remonstrating angrily with Stanley and is beaten up by him. Stanley's friends stop him from hitting his wife by dragging him into the bathroom. Stella seeks refuge in Eunice's apartment.	36:43–38:35
Scene 10	Standing in front of Eunice's apartment, Stanley keeps on shouting Stella's name. Although Eunice wants Stella to stay with her, she returns to Stanley.	38:36–41:51
Scene 11	Outraged at her sister's returning to Stanley, Blanche is calmed down by Mitch.	41:52–43:16
Scene 12	Blanche tries to persuade Stella into leaving Stanley. Stanley overhears Blanche's attempts to denigrate him by portraying him as a contemptible brute.	43:17–49:04
Scene 13	Stanley tells Blanche that a certain Mr. Shaw remembers meeting her at the disreputable hotel Flamingo in Laurel. Blanche denies this but looks terrified.	49:05–51:59
Scene 14	Stanley leaves, and Blanche tries to find out how much her sister knows about her past behaviour. Moreover, she tells Stella that she is on edge because Mitch is coming to take her out. Since she is afraid of getting old and being unable to attract Mitch, she has to be reassured by Stella.	52:00–56:36
Scene 15	Blanche is lounging in an armchair when the doorbell suddenly rings. A young man arrives to collect money for a paper.	56:37–1:00:29
Scene 16	Mitch arrives at Elysian Fields and takes Blanche to a dance casino. After leaving the dance casino, they are having a conversation on a pier in front of the dance casino. After Blanche has given Mitch insights into the death of her former husband, he proposes marriage to her.	1:00:30–1:12:34
Scene 17	Mitch and Stanley are about to get into a fight at their workplace, a factory.	1:12:35–1:13:05
Scene 18	The Kowalski apartment: Stanley informs Stella about Blanche's shady past and the fact that he has let Mitch in on Blanche's dark/well-kept secrets. On hearing about her sister's promiscuous behaviour, Stella is very upset. When she emerges from the bathroom and sees her sister, Blanche has a hunch that something is wrong.	1:13:06–1:17:55
Scene 19	Stanley, Stella and Blanche are sitting at a dinner table in the Kowalski apartment. Trying to conceal her disappointment at being stood up by Mitch, Blanche tries to appear cheerful and well-balanced. When Stella starts criticizing Stanley's table manners, he flies into a rage. When the disastrous birthday party is over, Blanche tries to call Mitch. In the meantime, Stanley makes up with Stella in front of the house.	1:17:56–1:21:54

Scene 20	On returning to the flat, Stanley gives Blanche a bus ticket back to Laurel. Stella is outraged at Stanley's callousness. Stanley and Stella's ensuing quarrel is interrupted by Stella's labour pains.	1:21:55–1:25:54
Scene 21	Blanche is alone in the Kowalski flat, drinking. Mitch arrives and accuses her of lying about her age and her innocence. Blanche tries in vain to explain herself. When Mitch tries to rape Blanche, her cries frighten him off. He rushes outside accompanied by Blanche's loud shrieks.	1:25:55–1:37:07
Scene 22	Blanche is alone in the Kowalski flat, drunk and half crazy. Stanley returns home and mocks Blanche's "fine feathers" and her illusions.	1:37:08–1:43:09
Scene 23	Blanche and Stanley start quarreling. He attacks her and throws her on her bed. After Stanley has let go of Blanche, she tries to call her old admirer Shep in order to ask for help.	1:43:10–1:46:32
Scene 24	Being obviously aroused by Blanche's fear, Stanley makes it clear that he desires to make love to her. When he approaches Blanche, a violent struggle ensues. Stanley finally manages to overpower and get hold of Blanche.	1:46:33–1:48:08
Scene 25	The Kowalski apartment: A subdued poker party is in progress. Stella is packing Blanche's belongings. Blanche emerges from the bathroom expecting to go on a cruise with her old admirer Shep.	1:48:09–1:52:04
Scene 26	A doctor and a matron from a hospital arrive at Elysian Fields. Blanche starts panicking and struggling. During Blanche's ordeal, Mitch tries to hit Stanley.	1:52:05–1:56:34
Scene 27	Feeling reassured by the doctor's kindness, Blanche leaves on his arm.	1:56:35–1:58:40
Scene 28	Carrying her baby in her arms, Stella declares that she will not return to Stanley. In the background, Stanley calls Stella's name.	1:58:41–1:59:17

4.1 Reflections on the qualities and necessities of a film version of *A Streetcar Named Desire*

Um die Schülerinnen und Schüler eingangs für Aspekte bzw. Kriterien zu sensibilisieren, die bei der Verfilmung des Dramas *A Streetcar Named Desire* von entscheidender Wichtigkeit sein können, erörtern sie zunächst im Rahmen eines Unterrichtsgesprächs folgende Fragestellungen:

> Do you think it is a good idea to make Williams' drama into a movie? Give reasons.
> Elia Kazan's film version of *A Streetcar Named Desire* was a huge box-office success in 1951. What might have been the reasons for the movie's success?

Während hinsichtlich der Beantwortung der ersten Frage ein weitgefächertes Spektrum individueller Antworten und Eindrücke zu erwarten ist, sollte im Rahmen der Beantwortung von Frage 2 mit Nachdruck darauf hingewirkt werden, dass die Schülerinnen und Schüler die von ihnen genannten Aspekte genau begründen.
Somit könnten unter anderem folgende Aspekte genannt werden:

- Kazan might have given roles to very talented or famous actors because a lot of moviegoers are very much attracted to the individual charisma of certain actors or actresses

- Kazan might have used a large number of special effects in order to excite and intrigue the audience
- he might have made use of close-ups on the actors' faces to give the audience insight into their feelings and inner turmoil
- he might have added a scene to enhance the original play's dramatic effect

Dem Umstand Rechnung tragend, dass Kazans Film eine sehr überschaubare Anzahl von Änderungen gegenüber dem Originalfilm aufweist, werden die Schülerinnen vor der Betrachtung der Anfangssequenz des Films mit einem Zitat des Kritikers Forster Hirsch konfrontiert, welches darauf anspielt, dass eine Filmversion eines Williams-Dramas notwendigerweise eng an die Dramenvorlage angelehnt sein muss. Somit ergeht folgender Arbeitsauftrag an die Lerngruppe:

Explain and comment on the following statement made by the critic Forster Hirsch: "A movie based on a Tennessee Williams play is a Tennessee Williams film."
What does Hirsch want to express?

Mögliche Schülerbeitrage können zum Zwecke einer größeren Transparenz im Rahmen der unterrichtlichen Diskussion an der Tafel festgehalten werden:

- a screen adaptation of a drama by T. Williams must not deviate from the drama's original plot lest it distort its spirit and message
- the director of a screen adaptation will be dependent on the cooperation of the playwright
- a Tennessee Williams drama already comprises the key components of an interesting, intriguing and successful movie

Unter dem Eindruck der im Rahmen des Unterrichtsgesprächs geäußerten Vermutungen und Einschätzungen wird den Schülerinnen und Schülern in einem nächsten Unterrichtsschritt die filmische Umsetzung von Blanches Ankunft in New Orleans bzw. Elysian Fields präsentiert (Scene 1–4, 0:1:13– 0:14:19). Da die genannte Sequenz, welche die erste Szene des Originaldramas umspannt, neben dem Verzicht auf Stanleys „Fleischwurf" auch einige entscheidende Änderungen hinsichtlich der Wahl von Orten bzw. Schauplätzen aufweist, sollten die Schülerinnen und Schüler dazu angehalten werden, die in den Filmszenen auftretenden Unterschiede zu benennen, zu bewerten und auf ihre Zweckmäßigkeit bzw. ihren Effekt hin zu untersuchen. Zu diesem Zweck betrachten die Schülerinnen und Schüler zunächst die Eingangssequenz des Films unter folgender Aufgabenstellung:

Watch the movie's introductory sequence and note down the differences that exist between the movie and the original play.

Nachdem die Schülerinnen und Schüler die ihnen aufgefallenen Unterschiede im Plenum benannt haben, wird ihnen ein Arbeitsblatt ausgehändigt, auf dem sechs wesentliche, von ihnen voraussichtlich bereits benannte Unterschiede aufgeführt sind. Die Aufgabe der Schülerinnen und Schüler besteht nun darin, die genannten Unterschiede zu analysieren bzw. zu bewerten (Copy 10).

The movie vs the drama

Analyse and evaluate the modifications that have been made to the movie by filling in the following worksheet.

Deviations from the play	Possible reasons for the deviations	Personal view (on the changes)
1. While the drama opens with Stanley heaving a package of meat at Stella, the movie dispenses with that particular incident. Instead, the movie opens with Blanche arriving at New Orleans central station and speaking the famous words: "They told me to take a streetcar named Desire ..." (0:02:06 – 0:02:14)		
2. In the movie, Blanche passes by a pub in which some drunks are getting into a fight. One of the drunks almost knocks against her. This particular incident is not mentioned in the drama. (0:02:41 – 0:02:42)		
3. Blanche and Stella's reunion does not take place in the Kowalski apartment, but in a bowling alley where Stanley and his friends shout, play and get into a fight. (0:04:46 – 0:05:02)		
4. The sisters' first talk about things that have happened during the time they haven't seen each other takes place in a restaurant. (0:05:12 – 0:07:03)		
5. During Blanche and Stanley's first encounter, a cat starts screeching. Blanche is not only given a start, but also clings to Stanley's strong arm – obviously in search of protection. (0:13:13 – 0:13:14)		
6. Stanley's question "You were married once, weren't you?" is echoed twice and the polka music that is ringing in Blanche's ears is also accompanied by an audible shot. (0:14:04 – 0:14:06)		

Hinsichtlich der Auseinandersetzung mit den möglichen Gründen (possible reasons) für die vorgenommenen Änderungen sollten die Schülerinnen und Schüler zu folgenden Ergebnissen gekommen sein:

Mögliche Lösungen zu *Copy 10*:

1. Apparently, Elia Kazan wants to make it clear that Blanche's personality and her development throughout the drama is the focus of his attention. In this connection, it is worth noting that the lines that are spoken by Blanche actually mark her development throughout the production.
2. Having omitted Stanley's throwing a package of meat at Stella, Kazan needs to find another incident that can illustrate the rudeness, coarseness and proletarian character of Blanche's new surroundings.
3. The bowling alley is a place that exudes crudeness, aggressiveness and life in a raw form. Thus, it also serves as a symbol of the savage and brutal forces of modern society.
4. It might be assumed that the nervous talk in the restaurant is intended to be a prelude to Blanche's violent outburst of temper in her sister's apartment. Thus, by keeping the audience in suspense, this particular change of location provides a heightened dramatic effect.
5. Apparently, Blanche's clinging to Stanley's arm is supposed to underscore her fragility and her need for protection. On the other hand, it might be a further hint at Blanche's secret attraction to the brute force that is personified by Stanley.
6. Kazan obviously wants to emphasize that Blanche is a traumatized person who is still affected by some very upsetting experiences she had in the past.

In der Absicht, die Aufmerksamkeit der Schülerinnen und Schüler auf den Umstand zu lenken, dass einige in Kazans Verfilmung vorgenommene Änderungen gegenüber dem Originaldrama nicht auf künstlerischen bzw. ästhetischen Erwägungen basieren, sondern auf die in den 50er-Jahren vorherrschende strenge Zensur zurückzuführen sind, wird in einem nächsten Unterrichtsschritt folgende Problematik im Plenum erörtert:

In the 1950s, the MPAA (Motion Picture Association of America) was a powerful organization that decided whether a movie had to undergo censorship or not. Joseph Breen, the MPAA's president, asked Kazan and Williams to make several changes to the script in order to meet the standards he demanded.
What modifications might have been expected to be made to the original play/script?

Mit folgenden Beiträgen/Vermutungen auf Seiten der Schüler könnte unter anderem zu rechnen sein:

- the rape of Blanche by Stanley has to be cut/omitted
- the homosexuality of Blanche's former husband has to be concealed
- offensive words such as "sugar-tit" (p. 47, l. 11) have to be edited out
- the sexual attraction between Stella and Stanley must not be too conspicuous

Auf Basis der genannten Vermutungen und in Vorbereitung auf die in der nächsten Unter-
richtsstunde anstehende Analyse tatsächlich aufgrund der Zensur vorgenommener Änderungen sollen sich die Schülerinnen und Schüler im Rahmen einer Hausaufgabe mit der Bedeutung der Zensur in Literatur und Film auseinandersetzen. Zu diesem Zweck bearbeiten sie
folgende Aufgabenstellung:

> Comment on the following statement: "Books or films that are sexually
> explicit or contain offensive language should either undergo censorship
> or should be banned."

4.2 Modifications made to the original script because of censorship

Der Analyse der wichtigsten im Film bzw. Filmskript vorgenommenen Änderungen gegenüber Williams Drama geht die Präsentation der von den Schülerinnen und Schülern im
Rahmen einer Hausaufgabe angefertigten Kommentare voran. Die Kommentare könnten
sich durch folgende Struktur bzw. Abwägungen auszeichnen:

> Often it depends on individual views, individual tastes or individual ex-
> periences whether a film/book is considered to be sexually explicit or
> not. Thus, films/books that are sexually explicit or contain offensive lan-
> guage should undergo censorship
>
> - if they feed anti-religious feelings
> - if they are racist
> - if they tend to discriminate against certain races, people or social
>   groups
>
> On the other hand, they should <u>not</u> undergo censorship
>
> - if sex or sexuality is used as a metaphor that hints at a hidden truth
> - if rude words or violent actions serve to create a realistic image of
>   people's behaviour
> - if the director intends to enlighten the audience as to new develop-
>   ments in society

Unmittelbar im Anschluss an die Präsentation der Kommentare wird den Schülerinnen und
Schülern die filmische Umsetzung der Dramenpassage vorgeführt, in der Blanche gegenüber
Mitch andeutet, dass sie sich am Selbstmord ihres homosexuellen Mannes Allan Grey schuldig
fühlt. Da die Filmszene nicht nur mit einem anderen Schauplatz aufwartet (Blanches und
Mitchs Unterhaltung findet auf dem Landungssteg vor einem Tanzlokal statt), sondern darüber
hinaus auch keinerlei Andeutungen hinsichtlich Allan Greys Homosexualität enthält, sollten
die Schülerinnen und Schüler in die Lage versetzt werden, Ursache und Wirkung der beiden
Änderungen zu analysieren bzw. zu bestimmen. Zu diesem Zweck wird das Betrachten der
genannten Filmszene (1:08:24 – 1:12:32) von folgendem Arbeitsauftrag begleitet:

> After reading the final part of scene 6 (pp. 102 – 104), watch the respec-
> tive film scene and note down all the modifications that have been made
> to the original play. What might have been the causes and effects of the
> changes that have been made? Point out the reasons for the changes
> and the (intended) effects.

Einzelne Schülerinnen und Schüler sollten die Ergebnisse auf Folie skizzieren und anschließend präsentieren.

First major change:
Kazan chooses a different setting for the scene. Mitch and Blanche's conversation does not take place in Stella's flat, but instead on the pier in front of a dance casino.

Reason for change:
The setting is reminiscent of the place where Allan Grey committed suicide.

(Intended) effect:
The whole ambience of the situation, the mist and the dim light, hardly revealing anything but the outlines of the actors, serves completely the purpose of illustrating that Blanche's mood is one of deep depression.

Second major change:
In the film scene, Blanche's monologue does not contain any words that hint at her husband's homosexuality. Adjectives such as "effeminate" and nouns such as "softness", which are used in the original play, are omitted. Moreover, Blanche does not talk about having discovered her husband in bed with another person. Instead, she gives a completely different reason for having killed him: "At night I pretended to sleep and I heard him crying. Crying the way a lost child cries ... That's why I killed him." (1:09:37 – 1:09:40)

Reason for change:
The scene has obviously undergone censorship. Allusions to Allan Grey's homosexuality had to be avoided.

Effect on the audience:
To those who have not read or seen the original play, Blanche's words might be misleading. They might think that Blanche's contempt for her husband was due to his lacking get-up and strength.

Third major change:
The words Blanche directs at her husband immediately before his suicide are different.
Instead of saying "You disgust me ...", she tells him "You're weak. I've lost respect for you. I despise you." (1:11:06 – 1:11:12)

Reason for change:
See second major change.

Effect on the audience:
For the mature audience, it might be obvious what is meant when Blanche concludes that she "has lost all respect for him (Allan)."

Für die Untersuchung der filmischen Umsetzung der Vergewaltigungsszene bietet sich eine ähnliche Vorgehensweise an wie bei der Untersuchung von Blanches Monolog in der Gegenwart Mitchs (siehe oben).

 After reading the final part of scene 10 (p. 145, l. 25 – p. 146), watch the respective film scene (1:46:36 – 1:48:14) and note down all the modifications that have been made to the original play. What are the causes and effects of the changes?

First major change:
Stanley's statement "We've had this date right from the beginning" is omitted (p. 146, ll. 25–26).

Reason for change:
The statement has obviously undergone censorship. Since the word date carries sexual connotations it had to be left out.

(Intended) effect:
Stanley's being too explicit about his intention to rape Blanche is meant to be avoided.

Second major change:
Immediately after Blanche's rape, a cut to a street cleaner's hose is inserted.

Reason for change:
The hose, which is a strong phallic symbol, is meant to hint at a sexual act that has just taken place.

(Intended) effect on the audience:
Blanche's rape by Stanley is revealed to the audience.

Dem Betrachten der augenfällig geänderten Schlussszene (Stella schwört, nicht mehr zu Stanley zurückkehren zu wollen, 1:58:56–1:59:04) soll schließlich ein reger und freier Austausch von Eindrücken und Meinungen im Plenum folgen. Die Unterrichtsdiskussion könnte durch folgende Impulse eingeleitet werden:

What might have been the reasons for the choice of a different ending?

Da die Schülerinnen und Schüler schon im Vorfeld für Aussagen und Andeutungen, welche in den 50er-Jahren gemeinhin der Zensur unterlagen, sensibilisiert worden sind, sollten sie folgende kausale Zusammenhänge herstellen können:

- Since Stanley has obviously raped Blanche and thus has committed a crime, a punishment has to be imposed upon him. In being left by Stella, he is given the chance of paying for his crime.
- If Stella was unwilling to leave Stanley, she would prove to be morally depraved and thus might set a bad example for the audience.
- Stanley's punishment makes Blanche's moral victory more noticeable.

Da das Betrachten und Analysieren der radikal geänderten Schlussszene auch eine willkommene Gelegenheit bietet, sich die Botschaft von Williams Drama zu vergegenwärtigen, diskutieren die Schülerinnen und Schüler schließlich folgende weitere Fragestellung im Plenum:

Does the movie's different ending distort the message of Williams' drama beyond all recognition? Give reasons.

Mit folgenden Schülerbeiträgen sollte zu rechnen sein:

- Since Williams' drama is based on the assumption that the desire for love and sex determines people's actions and plans, the movie's ending is not only entirely unsuitable, but also misleading.
- Since there is an immensely strong sexual attraction between Stella and Stanley, the movie's ending belies the true nature of their relationship.
- Taking into account that Stella, just like Blanche, needs someone she can cling to, someone that can take care of her and that she is attracted to, her intention to leave Stanley seems to lack credibility. Thus, the different ending masks her true character.

In der Absicht, die Schülerinnen und Schüler in die Lage zu versetzen, ihr im Unterrichtsgespräch unter Beweis gestelltes Wissen bzw. Gespür im Sinne eines Transfers fruchtbar zu machen, bearbeiten sie in einem nächsten Unterrichtsschritt folgende Kreativaufgabe:

Make up a dialogue between Elia Kazan and Joseph Breen. In the course of their conversation, Kazan wants to convince Breen of the necessity of making no changes to the text of Williams' original play and Breen, on the other hand, wants to convince Kazan of the necessity of changing the passages mentioned above.

In Vorbereitung auf die in der nächsten Stunde zu leistende Analyse einzelner Kameraeinstellungen und deren Funktion informieren sich die Schülerinnen und Schüler im Rahmen einer Hausaufgabe über die in der Filmsprache üblichen Fachbegriffe und widmen sich darüber hinaus folgender Kreativaufgabe:

Choose a passage/incident in Williams' play that strikes you as very impressive or important. Explain what you would do in order to illustrate its importance in the movie. (What shots, music, light, special effects, etc. would you use?)

4.3 Watching the complete movie

4.3.1 Four tell-tale scenes

Da sich die Schülerinnen und Schüler aller Voraussicht nach schon im Rahmen der Hausaufgabe intensiver mit der Verwendung verschiedener Kameraeinstellungen (*field sizes*) auseinandergesetzt haben, sollten sie für die Analyse einiger bemerkenswerter Einstellungen, die in Kazans Film vorgenommen werden, hinreichend gewappnet sein. Die auf dem nachfolgenden Arbeitsblatt (*Copy 11*) angesprochenen „shots" sind allesamt Szenen entnommen, die Details enthüllen, welche in Williams Drama nicht explizit benannt bzw. ausgeführt werden wie beispielsweise Mitchs versteckter Groll gegen seine Mutter. Somit schauen sich die Schülerinnen und Schüler die genannten Szenen separat an, um sie anschließend mithilfe eines Arbeitsblattes zu analysieren. Die der Bearbeitung des Arbeitsblatts zugrunde liegende Aufgabenstellung lautet wie folgt:

Watch the scenes that are depicted on the worksheet. Find out what cuts are used and explain their effect and function.

Four tell-tale scenes

Scenes	Shot(s)	Function/effect
1. Blanche asks Mitch if he loves his mother. (1:08:03 – 1:08:07)		
2. Mitch looks at Blanche's face, which is illuminated by the glare of a light bulb. (1:30:19 – 1:30:28)		
3. Giving in to Stanley's vociferous appeals, Stella descends the stairs leading from Eunice's apartment. (0:40:12 – 0:41:26)		
4. During the poker game in the Kowalski apartment, Eunice gets worked up about the noise that is being made by the poker players. (0:28:22 – 0:29:14)		

Lösungsvorschläge zu *Copy 11*:

1.
Shot: Mitch's face is shot in close-up.

Function/effect: Pulling a wry face, nodding hesitantly and avoiding the word "yes" suggest that he does not actually love his mother; for she is the one who has constantly hemmed him in and, what is more, has prevented him from having amorous experiences like, for example, his friend Stanley.

2.
Shot: Blanche's face is shot in close-up.

Function/effect: The camera reveals all signs of age, every wrinkle can be observed in the bright spotlight.

3.
Shot: The camera cuts back and forth between Stella and Stanley. While Stanley's face is shot in close-up, there are long shots of Stella's descent.

Function/effect: The close-ups of Stanley's face underscore his desperation and his passion for Stella. Since Stella is meant to be represented as a woman who is morally superior to Stanley (see movie's ending), her passion for her husband has to be concealed.

4.
Shot: The camera cuts back and forth between the Kowalski and Hubbel apartment (medium long shots).

Function/effect: By moving the camera fluidly throughout the whole apartment, Kazan gives the audience an insight into the stifling restriction that its usual inhabitants (and Blanche) are exposed to.

4.3.2 More details and striking differences

Zum Abschluss der Unterrichtsreihe schauen die Schülerinnen und Schüler sich schließlich den kompletten Film an. Um die in den vorangegangenen Unterrichtsschritten erworbenen Kenntnisse fruchtbar zu machen, wird das Schauen des Films durch das Bearbeiten eines Arbeitsblattes (*Copy 12*) begleitet. Hierbei werden die Schülerinnen und Schüler nicht nur in die Lage versetzt, ihre Sensibilisierung für Abweichungen von der Dramenvorlage unter Beweis zu stellen, sondern ihnen wird darüber hinaus auch die Möglichkeit eingeräumt, Bewertungen hinsichtlich der schauspielerischen Darbietungen vorzunehmen. Somit ergeht abschließend folgender Arbeitsauftrag an die Lerngruppe:

 Watch the movie and fill in the following worksheet.

Further differences and evaluation

I. Further differences between the original play and the movie

1. Additions:

_____

_____

_____

_____

Possible reasons:

_____

_____

_____

_____

2. Omissions:

_____

_____

_____

_____

Possible reasons:

_____

_____

_____

_____

3. General differences:

_____

_____

_____

_____

II. Evaluation of the principal actors and actresses

1. Marlon Brando (Stanley)

_____

_____

_____

_____

2. Vivien Leigh (Blanche)

_____

_____

_____

_____

3. Karl Malden (Mitch)

_____

_____

_____

_____

4. Kim Hunter (Stella)

_____

_____

_____

_____

Neben den individuellen Eindrücken, welche die Schülerinnen und Schüler bei der Bearbeitung des zweiten Teils des Arbeitsblattes artikulieren, sollten bei der Bearbeitung des ersten Aufgabenteils unter anderem folgende verbindliche Angaben gemacht werden:

Additions:

1. A scene in which Stanley and Mitch are about to get into a fight at their workplace (1:12:35 – 1:12:54).

   Possible reason for the addition:
   Since Blanche has given Mitch a new lease of life, it must have been a very upsetting experience for him to learn that her past is overshadowed by promiscuous behaviour. Thus, the scene serves to underscore Mitch's disappointment and anger at being robbed of a future with a "straight" woman.
   Forming a stark contrast to the preceding scene in which Mitch proposed marriage to Blanche, this particular scene also has a tremendous dramatic effect.

2. Blanche reacts to Mitch's exclamation "I thought you were straight!" by answering "A line can be straight or a street. But the heart of a human being ...?" (1:32:47 – 1:32:58)

   Possible reasons for the addition:
   By inserting this line Kazan underscores Blanche's contempt for moralizers and those who seize the moral high ground.

   Omissions:
   When informing Stella about Blanche's shady past in the original play, Stanley says things such as "Boy, oh, boy, I'd like to have been in that office when Dame Blanche was called on the carpet!" (p. 110, ll. 20 – 22). The film version does not contain comparable sentences.

   Possible reason for the omission:
   Kazan apparently wants to draw attention to Stanley's hidden sensitivity. Knowing that his revelations about Blanche's shady past might hurt or provoke Stella, he tries to avoid adding fuel to the fire by giving his words an air of triumphalism.

Abschließend bietet es sich an, die Schülerinnen und Schüler im Rahmen einer Hausaufgabe eine Filmkritik verfassen zu lassen.

Anhang

1. Literaturhinweise

- **Tennessee Williams**

  - Ronald Hayman, *Tennessee Williams: Everyone Else Is an Audience*, Yale University Press, New York and London 1985

  - Donald Spoto, *The Kindness of Strangers: The Life of Tennessee Williams*, Bodley Head, London 1985

- *A Streetcar Named Desire*

  - Philip C. Kolin (ed.), *Confronting Tennessee William's A Streetcar Named Desire* (Contributions in Drama and Theatre Studies, No 50), Greenwood Press, Westport, Connecticut 1993

  - Nancy M. Tischler, *Student Companion to Tennessee Williams*, Greenwood Press, West-port, Connecticut 2000

2. Internetadressen

- **zum Drama**

  Konzise und praktische Informationen zum Drama *A Streetcar Named Desire*:

  - www.gradesaver.com/classicnotes/titles/desire/section3.html

  - www.school-scout.de/2527/tennessee-williams-a-streetcar-named-desire

  - www.sparknotes.com/lit/streetcar

- **zu den Verfilmungen**

  Bildmaterial und Informationen über Verfilmungen:

  - www.filmsite.org/stre.html

  - www.imdb.com/title/tt0044081

  - www.starpulse.com/Movies/Streetcar_Named_Desire,_A

  - www.timeout.com/film/newyork/reviews/75483/A_Streetcar_Named_Desire.html

Edited by Hans Kröger

EINFACH ENGLISCH

Bend it Like Beckham

Unterrichtsmodell · Schöningh

Fordern Sie unseren Prospekt zur Reihe an:
Informationen zum Nulltarif ℂ 08 00 / 1 81 87 87

SCHÖNINGH VERLAG
Postfach 2540 · 33055 Paderborn

Schöningh

E-Mail: info@schoeningh.de
Internet: www.schoeningh-schulbuch.de